PERTH THEN AND NOW

You can find most of the sites featured in the

8 St Georges Terrace
10 T&G Chambers / Citibank House
12 Government (Stirling) Gardens
14 The Weld Club
16 Old Court House
18 Commissariat Stores / Supreme Court
20 Esplanade Kiosk
22 Perth City Baths
24 Esplanade Reserve / Elizabeth Quay
26 Capitol Theatre / Temple Court
28 Freemason's Hotel / Palace Hotel
30 AMP Chambers
32 Newspaper House
34 Perth Boys' School
36 Bishop Hale's School / The Cloisters
38 Pensioner Barracks
40 Perth Observatory
42 Perth Park / Kings Park
44 State War Memorial
46 Leake Memorial, Kings Park
48 Market Gardens, Mounts Bay Road
50 Melbourne Hotel
52 Perth Entertainment Centre
54 Russell Square
56 Great Western Hotel
58 Horseshoe Bridge
60 City Markets
62 Wesley Church
64 His Majesty's Theatre
66 Hay Street Tramline Construction

74 General Post Office Building
76 Perth Railway Station
78 Perth Boys' School / PICA
80 Western Australian Museum
82 Swan Barracks
84 Trades Hall
86 Barrack Street Bridge
88 Barrack Street
90 Twiss Street (Hay Street)
92 Theatre Royal & Hotel Metropole
94 Ambassadors Theatre
96 Perth Town Hall
98 Barrack Street from the Town Hall
100 Central Government Offices
102 St George's Chambers
104 St George's Cathedral
106 Government House
108 Langley Park
110 Causeway Bridge
112 The WACA
114 Claise Brook
116 St Mary's Cathedral
118 St George's Hall
124 Old Mill, South Perth
126 Narrows Bridge
128 Old Swan Brewery

Numbers in red circles refer to the pages where sites appear in the book.

* The map is intended to give readers a broad view of where the sites are located. Please consult a tourist map for greater detail.

PERTH

THEN AND NOW®

First published in the United Kingdom in 2016 by
PAVILION BOOKS
an imprint of Pavilion Books Company Ltd.
43 Great Ormond Street
London WC1N 3HZ

"Then and Now" is a registered trademark of Salamander Books Limited,
a division of Pavilion Books Group.

ISBN-13: 978-1-910904-90-9

Repro by Rival Colour, UK.
Printed by 1010 Printing International Ltd, China.

Reprinted 2016, 2017, 2019

ACKNOWLEDGEMENTS
A book like this could not be produced without the help of a great many people behind the
scenes and I would like to particularly thank the ever friendly staff at the State Library of
Western Australia and the Perth History Centre, who always answer my 'need to know yesterday'
questions promptly and efficiently. Thanks also go to the Royal Western Australian Historical
Society for allowing me access to their unique collections and, last but not least, to the City of
Perth and board of Heritage Perth, without whose encouragement and support I would not have
been able to immerse myself in the amazing history of this beautiful city for the last 10 years.

PICTURE CREDITS

Then Photographs:
All photographs are courtesy of the State Library of Western Australia, except for those on
the following pages: 10 right, 66, 68 left, 96, 100 top, 126 top (courtesy of the Royal Western
Australian Historical Society), 108 (courtesy of the Aviation Heritage Museum of WA).

Now Photographs:
All photographs were taken by David Watts with the exception of those on the following pages:
49, 69 top, 129 (Richard Offen), 59 bottom (Evad37), 113 (Getty Images).

PERTH

THEN AND NOW®

RICHARD OFFEN

PAVILION

St Georges Terrace, 1905   p. 8

The Weld Club, c. 1893   p. 14

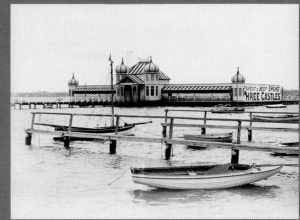

Perth City Baths, 1899   p. 22

Capitol Theatre and Temple Court, 1930   p. 26

Freemason's Hotel, c. 1890   p. 28

Pensioner Barracks, c. 1866   p. 38

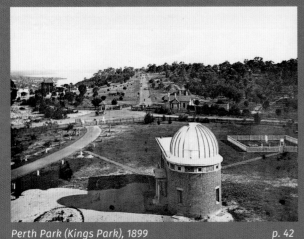

Perth Park (Kings Park), 1899   p. 42

Market Gardens at Mounts Bay Road, 1905   p. 48

Perth Entertainment Centre, 1974   p. 52

Great Western Hotel, c. 1897 p. 56

Horseshoe Bridge, 1905 p. 58

General Post Office Building, c. 1930 p. 74

Barrack Street, 1901 p. 88

Ambassadors Theatre, 1929 p. 94

Central Government Offices, c. 1879 p. 100

The WACA, c. 1905 p. 112

Old Swan Brewery, c. 1910 p. 128

Winthrop Hall, 1932 p. 134

PERTH
THEN AND NOW INTRODUCTION

'The Swan River would require the language of a poet to describe it. The scenery on its banks is lovely beyond description; its course is beautifully serpentine.' So wrote one correspondent in a letter to the *Glasgow Courier* sent from the HMS *Sulphur*, moored in Cockburn Sound, in September 1829.

Sadly, for the settlers who formed the Swan River Colony in the winter of 1829, it was soon discovered that the vast river floodplain was nothing more than a huge and agriculturally useless sand dune. Such were the many and severe hardships suffered by those early settlers that one of their number, Eliza Shaw, was moved to suggest, 'The man who declared this country good deserves hanging nine times over.'

The beauty and usefulness of the river on which Perth now stands has been recognised for many millennia. Archaeological evidence shows that Aboriginal people have been using the Swan River and its surrounds as an important source of food for at least 40,000 years. As a result, the area also became an important cultural meeting place for the Whadjuk Noongar people, who have gathered here for many thousands of years.

Although Europeans had known about the west coast of Australia for several centuries, early expeditions had claimed only the eastern half of the continent. It was some years after the formation of the British colony in New South Wales before an interest was taken in the western seaboard. This was primarily brought about in the wake of the Napoleonic Wars, when intelligence information suggested that other nations were taking a more than passing interest in the western half of Australia. After years of conflict at home, the British were keen to avoid the prospect of French neighbours in the Antipodes.

After making a first unsteady British foothold on the southern coast in Albany, in 1827 Captain James Stirling was despatched to explore the west coast for a suitable settlement. Having spent 12 days exploring the Swan River area, he was beguiled by its beauty and misled by the lushness of the flora into believing it was similar to the most fertile parts of Italy. Seeing only the possibilities and the prospects for new settlement, the foundations of Perth were laid.

Named after the birthplace of Lord Murray, the British Parliament's Colonial Secretary, Perth gradually took shape as a town despite the problems of sourcing suitable building materials. This meant that many were still sleeping in tents long after the declaration of the township. In addition to the sparsity of agricultural land, two other problems hampered progress. One was an acute lack of labour to carry out the construction of infrastructure such as roads and bridges; the other was a severe shortage of capital investment.

It had always been intended for Western Australia to be a free settlement rather than a penal colony, but farmers and landowners saw the potential for convicts to be a source of cheap labour. After a considerable amount of political lobbying, and much to the surprise of those intended as their gaolers, the first convicts arrived in June 1850 – the irony being that the ship carrying the first cargo of convicts had overtaken the one carrying the British Government message confirming its approval for transportation to start.

This influx of labour, some of it skilled, soon transformed Perth and helped build public buildings such as the Town Hall, the first Colonial School and Government House. With the convicts came experienced professionals, employed to oversee the projects undertaken by them. One was Richard Roach Jewell, the first trained architect in the colony, who has left us a legacy of many elegant buildings from his drawing board, the principal ones of which appear in the pages of this book.

By 1856, when Perth was declared a city by Queen Victoria, its physical and social shape had largely been determined. The administrative, political and business centre was based around St Georges Terrace; Hay and Murray Streets developed as a commercial and shopping precinct; while further west around Kings Street and also in East Perth, artisans' workshops, cottages and stockyards were to be found.

Still vital for communications was the river. A port was developed at the southern end of William Street, providing a trading link with the sea port at Fremantle and the agricultural community of the Swan Valley at Guildford.

Economic activity at this time was still based on agriculture, with wool a primary export for many years, aided by exploiting newly found resources such as sandalwood. Income was scarce, however, and the colony struggled to make its mark until the end of the 19th century when Western Australia struck gold and the first resource boom began.

With the 1890s discovery of gold in the Murchison and Eastern Goldfields, Perth witnessed a massive influx of population and wealth. The gold rush brought about a transformation from modest country town to prosperous commercial city, demonstrated by the grandeur of the former Land Titles Building, the graceful lines of the McNess Royal Arcade and the opulence of His Majesty's Theatre, all erected to demonstrate Perth's status as a significant gold city.

In 1901 Federation transformed Western Australia from an independent colony to a State of the Commonwealth of Australia, and Perth gained the status of capital city for the new state. During the 1920s the appearance and character of Perth was confirmed rather than altered, although late in the 1930s the construction of several multi-storey buildings in the city centre, such as the Gledden, CMLA and Commonwealth Bank buildings, were a portent of the dramatic changes the city would undergo in the last 40 years of the 20th century.

The population of Perth changed in size and character after World War II as immigration brought new cultures and traditions to the city. A major phase of development spurred on by further resource booms of the 1960s, 70s and 80s saw skyscrapers built and the city take on a more modern character, sometimes in ways which we would now have cause to question. During the entrepreneurial 1980s and more temperate 1990s, the city continued its transition from a Victorian gold town into a dynamic and progressive city.

From very humble and difficult beginnings, Perth has evolved into an exciting and beautiful cosmopolitan city, full of evidence of its past and promises for its future. This book charts some of that evolution, reveals the layers created by the city's development and touches on some of the characters who have made Perth the bewitching place it is today.

1905

ST GEORGES TERRACE

The fashionable residential and business area of town

ABOVE: This street was initially called 'King George's Terrace', after King George IV, but by the time the English geographer John Arrowsmith drew a map of the town in 1833, it was being referred to as 'St George's Terrace', probably being renamed after the king's death in 1830. To ensure standards were maintained, a regulation was passed in 1833, which stipulated that only homes costing at least £200 could be built on this street and it became a fashionable residential and business area of the town. Various improvements to the street were carried out in the 1870s and 80s, including levelling and the addition of a footpath, but it was the new-found gold wealth of the 1890s that changed the architecture of the street out of all recognition and removed most of the residential properties. On the immediate left of the photograph stands the United Services Hotel and on the right is Weld Chambers, containing the Trade Protection Association.

ABOVE: Following the first gold boom and during the Great Depression of the 1930s, few changes were made to the late 19th-century elegance of 'the Terrace' (as it is locally known), but the Western Australian mineral boom, which started after World War II, was to change all that. A need for a significant increase in office accommodation, coupled with an internationally held disregard for the significance of 19th-century architecture, brought about the disappearance of buildings which today would be considered important examples of their time. The United Services Hotel was replaced in the early 1970s by the Suncorp building and Weld Chambers made way for the St Martins Centre in 1978. At about the same time, the street name also lost its apostrophe. While the 19th-century charm of the western end of the street has disappeared, the area has retained the bustling atmosphere of a busy central business district.

1928

T&G CHAMBERS / CITIBANK HOUSE

The elegant T&G Chambers survived until 1960

LEFT: Prior to the construction of T&G Chambers in 1897, the site was occupied by two buildings: the National Bank of Australasia and the United Service Tavern Hotel. In the early days of the Swan River Colony there was insufficient collateral to start a bank and it was not until 1837 that the Bank of Western Australia opened, followed in 1841 by the National Bank of Australasia, which opened a branch on the corner of St Georges Terrace and Barrack Street. This building survived until it was purchased by the Temperance & General Life Assurance Company, who commissioned architect J.J. Talbot Hobbs to design their new offices. At the back of the building was the headquarters of the Women's Christian Temperance Union, which was founded in 1892 to create a 'sober and pure world'.

BELOW: The first buildings on the plot: the National Bank of Australasia and the United Service Tavern Hotel (far right) occupied the site until 1897.

c. 1870

RIGHT: The gracefully elegant T&G Chambers survived until 1960, when the need for more office space drove the owners to demolish the building and construct what was for some 10 years the tallest building in central Perth. Construction of the new, steel-framed building was not without problems, as the high water table in the area demanded raft-type foundations. When it opened in 1962 it was known as the T&G Building but changed its name to Citibank House after the bank became its sole occupier. By the 1980s, the building was in need of modernisation. Planning constraints meant it was not viable to demolish and rebuild once again, so an extensive refurbishment scheme was developed which involved completely changing the external appearance of the building. Of the buildings that once encircled the junction of Barrack Street and St Georges Terrace, only the State Buildings remain as a reminder of past architectural styles, the rest show evidence of a thriving, modern commercial city.

1885

GOVERNMENT GARDENS / STIRLING GARDENS

Perth's first public garden seen from the Town Hall's clock tower

ABOVE: Almost immediately after the foundation of Perth in August 1829, the Scottish-born naturalist James Drummond set up a 'naturalisation garden' within what would become Stirling Gardens. Here Drummond planted the seeds of various food crops brought with him from England in order to discover what would and would not grow successfully in this unknown climate. In addition to the vegetable and fruit varieties Drummond propagated, he also planted some acorns from which two oak trees, still to be seen in the garden, grew. The garden was gazetted as a botanical garden in 1845, becoming Perth's first public garden. A year later it was leased to Henry Cole, before returning to government control in 1856. The Governor's jetty can be clearly seen on the left side of the photograph. In the foreground are the early sections of Central Government Offices and beyond the gardens are the Court House (left) and the Commissariat Stores (right).

ABOVE: The park continued to be the city's botanic gardens until 1962 when the nearby Kings Park Botanic Gardens were officially established. Government Gardens (renamed Stirling Gardens in 1979) were redesigned in 1965 by the City of Perth Parks and Gardens Department, using Toodyay stone for retaining walls and shallow pools, one of which has a much photographed group of bronze kangaroos at the water's edge. The garden also features other sculptures such as the statue of Alexander Forrest (1849–1901), a prominent Western Australian explorer, politician and Mayor of Perth. Other features include the Holocaust Memorial and (visible behind the lamp-post on the left) *Harmony of Minerals*, an ore obelisk erected in 1971. The obelisk consists of a 14-metre (46-foot) oil drill pipe on which have been threaded 15 different Western Australian ores representing the natural wealth of the state. On the left of the photograph is the corner of the 1963 Council House office block, while over the roof of the Central Government Offices, by the river, is the glass spire of the Bell Tower (also known as Swan Bells), which opened in 2000 as part of Western Australia's millennium celebrations. Drummond's original oak trees can still be found among the central block of trees in this picture.

THE WELD CLUB

An exclusive gentlemen's club since 1871

BELOW: The Weld Club was founded in 1871 as an exclusive gentlemen's club named after Frederick Weld, Governor of Western Australia from 1869 to 1875. The club's members, who were from the upper echelons of Perth society, met to discuss politics, play billiards, invest in an informal stock exchange and read the latest news in British newspapers. Initially meeting in two houses on St Georges Terrace, the club decided in 1890 to build a much larger clubhouse on a prestigious block of land on the corner of the Esplanade and Barrack Street, which had previously been occupied by the home of the Dean of St George's Cathedral. A design competition was held and the winner, J. J. Talbot Hobbs, created a two-storey building, which was officially opened in December 1892.

c. 1893

WELD CLUB PERTH W.A.

BELOW: By the beginning of the 20th century the club had grown sufficiently for a large extension, which was built especially for country members who required accommodation when visiting the city. An extension, which doubled the size of the club, was opened at the end of 1904. In 1985 a restoration plan for the building was funded by leasing some of the club's land to create Exchange Plaza, a high-rise office development housing the Australian Securities Exchange. Although it is now dwarfed by this 40-storey development, the Weld Club continues to operate out of its historic premises. Described in 1892 as a 'unique centre of sociability' allowing for 'pleasant contact with everybody who is anybody in the small capital of the largest colony', this exclusive, male-only private club continues to thrive.

OLD COURT HOUSE
The oldest building in central Perth

16

LEFT: Soon after the first Swan River Colony settlers arrived, James Stirling issued a proclamation declaring that British statute law and common law would apply to the new colony, with Stirling initially the sole arbitrator. At first, court was held in the Rush Church on the corner of Hay and Irwin Streets, but by 1836 it moved into a courthouse designed by Henry Reveley. The building was described as 'chaste and appropriate' and cost £698 to build. The first Court of General Quarter Sessions was held there on 2 January 1837. For the first few years of its life, the building not only served as a court room but also the colony's theatre, concert hall, school and church. The Perth Drill Hall (with the curved roof) was built next door in 1896 as a response to a perceived need for better military training in the state.

ABOVE: Now the oldest-standing building in Perth, the courthouse was initially the only public building capable of accommodating large gatherings. As a result, in its early days it also functioned as an immigration depot and community centre. As the colony grew, so did the workload of the court, which often sat for 18 hours a day. In 1841 it was reported in the *Perth Gazette* that a criminal trial ended at 3 a.m., only after the accused had roused the jury to listen to his defence. By 1879 the case load became impossible to accommodate and judicial matters transferred to the neighbouring Commissariat Stores. From 1905 until 1965 the building was used by the Arbitration Court. It became home to the Law Society of Western Australia from 1965 to 1987 and was later opened to the public as a museum. The Old Court House Law Museum is now open from Tuesday to Friday weekly. The drill hall next door was demolished to provide extra parking for the Old Court House.

1890s

COMMISSARIAT STORES / SUPREME COURT

Site of the highest state court in Western Australia

ABOVE: Among the most important permanent buildings required by the fledgling Swan River Colony was a Commissariat Store in which to keep government supplies. Like the Old Court House, this building was designed by Henry Reveley and completed in July 1835. It had a large door opening on to the river, from which supplies could be transferred from river boats, with a grander, classical portico on the other side of the building as the main entrance. The building continued as stores until it was converted into a court building in 1879. However, working conditions in the former store were not comfortable, with complaints continually being made to the Legislative Council about how cold it was in winter and stuffy in summer. Parliamentary debate about the need, or not, for new law courts dragged on throughout the 1890s, with no firm conclusion being reached.

1861

RIGHT: The Commissariat Stores taken from the south side in 1861. The old police lock-up, Old Court House and Government House can be seen to the right.

ABOVE: The death knell for the Commissariat Stores was finally sounded in 1898 when it came to light that deliberations in the jury room could be overheard in other parts of the poorly adapted building. In 1901 plans were made to construct a new Supreme Court building on the site of the Stores, which would reclaim a section of the river to create a new public park. The new building was designed by the principal architect of the Public Works Department, John Grainger (father of composer Percy Grainger). Soon after work began, difficulties were encountered with the quality of building materials, which incurred much criticism in the local press and a Royal Commission was appointed to look into the problem. The matter settled, a foundation stone was laid in June 1902 and the building's official opening took place amid much pomp and ceremony a year later. The building is still home to the Supreme Court, the highest state court in Western Australia.

1929

ESPLANADE KIOSK

Dismantled, stored and rebuilt on an artificial island

ABOVE: In 1885 a pavilion and grandstand were built on the Esplanade Recreation Ground at a cost of £235. The grandstand was used for sporting and community events; one such event being the granting of responsible government to Western Australia, which was proclaimed on the Esplanade in 1890 and witnessed by a crowd of 6,000. In 1928 the grandstand was demolished and a refreshment kiosk, with public toilets and changing rooms, was built. Designed by Louis Bowser, a distinctive feature of the Arts and Crafts-style building was its interlocking octagonal structures. In addition to the changing rooms used by participants in the many sporting activities which took place on the Esplanade Reserves, the kiosk operated as a tea room and became popular for myriad social functions. At one stage it was the headquarters of the Old Contemptibles' (the British Expeditionary Force of 1914) Association.

ABOVE: The kiosk continued to serve the many sports clubs who had their facilities on the Esplanade until 1977, when it was converted into Annabella's Nightclub. However, this was not popular with residents in a nearby apartment block, who bombarded the city council with complaints about noise and rowdy behaviour, which eventually caused the nightclub to close in 1980. The building went on to be used by the Florence Hummerston Day Care Centre (named after the first woman elected to the Perth City Council) before being converted into a Chinese restaurant in 1998. To make way for the construction of Elizabeth Quay between 2012 and 2016, the Esplanade Kiosk was dismantled brick by brick and stored off-site. It has now been reconstructed on an artificial island in the quay inlet where it is once again being used as a restaurant.

PERTH CITY BATHS

Perth's first swimming pool

BELOW: With a climate conducive to the sport, swimming in the Swan River was popular from the very beginning of British colonisation. In the 1870s the need for a proper public bathing facility was discussed and a tin shed and water enclosure was eventually erected between Barrack and William Street jetties. This led to what one newspaper described as 'unrefined behaviour' by swimmers, who paid 'un-costumed visits to the mainland'. To alleviate the problem, the Police Act of 1892 prohibited bathing in a public place, 'except in proper costume', between 6 a.m. and 8 p.m. A Perth Bathing House Fund was established and the City Baths were built at a cost of £2,600 in 1898. The ornate Moorish Revival structure was designed by G.R. Johnson. The view in this photo shows a fledgling South Perth in the background.

1899

BELOW: The muddy river bed, combined with a frequent lack of deep water, meant that the City Baths were never very popular. Following the opening of the Crawley Baths in 1914, the City Baths were partially demolished and completely removed in 1920. The creation of Riverside Drive in 1937 effectively divided the area where the entrance to the baths was from the Esplanade Reserve. With the advent of the Elizabeth Quay project, which was completed in 2016, the area where the baths used to stand became part of the new river inlet, once again uniting Perth citizens with that part of the river.

Until the 1890s, much of the foreshore on the south side of the river was used for horticultural purposes. The opening of the Royal Perth Golf Club in 1895 and Perth Zoo in 1898, plus the addition of a ferry service, encouraged urbanisation and South Perth was declared a municipality in 1902. The new footbridge over the inlet entrance makes a graceful centrepiece between the re-sited Esplanade Kiosk on the left and the new ferry terminal opposite.

1898

ESPLANADE RESERVE / ELIZABETH QUAY

The Esplanade was open for sporting events, public gatherings and 'moral amusements'

ABOVE: The Esplanade Reserve was reclaimed from the river as part of a city council scheme to provide more spaces for 'moral amusements and manly sports'. Work to create new land between Barrack and William Street jetties began in 1873 and was completed in the early 1880s, when soil removed to level St Georges Terrace was added. Initially, an open drain running down Sherwood Court made the ground a very unpleasant place to be, but once this had been covered in, a Recreation Ground was opened in 1885. The event taking place in this photo from 1898 is a celebration of Queen Victoria's 79th birthday, attended by over 6,000 people. In the background is the ornate City Baths (centre), the clubhouse of Perth Yacht Club (far right) and a very sparsely populated South Perth in the distance.

ABOVE: By the beginning of the 20th century, the Recreation Ground was home to the Metropolitan Cricket Club, Perth Bowling Club, tennis courts and Perth Yacht Club. The ground also became the venue for many civic and national ceremonies, such as the celebration of Australian Federation on 1 January 1901. With some alterations in the 1920s, the Esplanade remained as popular as ever for sporting and cultural events. During the last decade of the 20th century a number of plans were suggested for the redevelopment of the Esplanade in order to 'reconnect' the city-centre with its river. In 2011 the State Government announced a scheme for the creation of Elizabeth Quay, to provide a waterside amenity including an inlet from the river, a pedestrian and cyclists' bridge and other leisure facilities. Elizabeth Quay was officially opened on 29 January 2016, with *Spanda*, a rippling water-inspired sculpture as its centrepiece. Eventually, the empty areas will be occupied by high-rise buildings that will dwarf the Bell Tower (Swan Bells) on the left of the photograph. South Perth, on the opposite side of the river, has grown considerably since the earlier photograph was taken. The photograph on the right was taken from the top of the Atlas Building on the Esplanade.

1930

CAPITOL THEATRE AND TEMPLE COURT CABARET
Two popular entertainment venues at the southern end of William Street

ABOVE: Designed by George Temple-Poole and Christian Mouritzen, the Art Nouveau Capitol Theatre (left) was opened in May 1929 and was the first in Australia with RCA Photophone – a sound-on-film system used for early 'talkies'. Other features of the cinema included a huge illuminated sign on the roof and a bust of the late Rudolph Valentino in the dress circle foyer, said to have permanently red lips from the kisses of fans. Another novel convenience offered by the theatre was a free bus service. The theatre's neighbour, the Temple Court Cabaret, was opened the same year on the corner of William Street and the Esplanade. It was a mixed-use building that included a theatre as well as a car park, tea room and offices. According to newspaper reports, it cost £250,000 to build and sent its developers into receivership soon after opening.

ABOVE: Although it had a reputation for having appalling acoustics, in the 1930s the Capitol Theatre became the main concert venue in Perth and home of the West Australian Symphony Orchestra, until they moved to the ABC's Basil Kirke Studios in the early 1960s. It also became a popular venue for political meetings and formal state and city functions. In 1966 the theatre was purchased by entrepreneur and later Lord Mayor, Thomas Wardle, who sold it two years later, after which it was demolished. Following its financial difficulties, the Temple Court Cabaret, then sharing its building with Sydney Atkinson Motors, was relaunched in 1933 as the Embassy Ballroom, which, with its magnificent décor, became a very well-frequented dance venue right up until its demolition in 1984 to make way for Wesfarmers House office block.

c. 1890

FREEMASON'S HOTEL / PALACE HOTEL
The first licenced hostelry in central Perth

ABOVE: The King's Head Hotel, the first licenced hostelry in central Perth, was opened on the corner of William Street and St Georges Terrace by William Dixon in 1830. A year later Dixon reassigned the property to William Leeder and it became known as Leeders Hotel, which was popular with gentlemen settlers and military officers. The scene of many grand dinners and celebrations, the building was extended in 1845, by which time it was referred to as the Freemason's Tavern, as it accommodated the first Masonic lodge in Western Australia. Still in the ownership of William Leeder's widow, fire destroyed several outbuildings at the rear of the property in 1888, by which time it was said to be in a dilapidated state. When this early 1890s photo was taken the reopened hotel, bar and luncheon room was being managed by a W.S. Savage.

ABOVE: The hotel was sold in 1894 to John De Baun, an American property investor and hotelier, who engaged architects to design a new hotel of the highest quality. No expense was spared in gathering the best materials from around the world to create the luxury establishment. The Palace Hotel, as it was renamed, proudly boasted 'electric light and gas laid on in every room'. The Commonwealth Banking Corporation purchased the property in 1972 and announced it was to be demolished. This caused a public campaign for the building's preservation, which was led by a group known as the Palace Guards. In 1978 the Bond Corporation purchased the property and adjacent ones, building the 50-storey office block which sits on the northeast corner of the building. Much of the original hotel survived this addition and was used as a bank. In 2015–2016 the old building underwent an extensive renovations program and was converted into offices.

1970

AMP CHAMBERS

The magnificent edifice on the corner of St Georges Terrace and William Street was lost to the wrecking ball in 1972

LEFT: The Australian Mutual Provident Society purchased the corner of St Georges Terrace and William Street in 1910 and in 1915 began to erect a six-storey, sandstone-clad building designed by the local architectural firm Oldham and Cox. Not only was the exterior an exuberant example of first gold rush Perth architecture, but the interior was finely detailed with jarrah panelling and carving. The crowning glory of the building was an iconic bronze statue, which became a landmark in central Perth. Weighing around 900 kilograms (1,985 pounds), the 3.7-metre (12-foot) high statue depicted four figures, the central one, symbolising Protection, was flanked by a man, woman and child.

RIGHT: In 1972 AMP announced plans to demolish the building and replace it with a modern skyscraper. The National Trust did not classify the old building, believing that the open space created in the new forecourt would greatly enhance the area. Although the building was not saved from demolition, the statue was purchased by millionaire collector Lew Whiteman. AMP later tried to buy the statue back from Whiteman, who said they did not deserve it. After Whiteman's death, the statue was sold at auction and can now be seen on the banks of Heardsman's Lake, west of Perth (see below). The new skyscraper was completed in 1975 and at 131 metres (430 feet) had the distinction of being the tallest office block in Perth, until Allendale Square, at 132 metres (433 feet), beat it a year later. The tower was renamed 140 St Georges Terrace after AMP moved out in 2002. Today the tower block is home to over 30 companies.

1932

NEWSPAPER HOUSE 'Meet you at the clock' meant only one building for Perth's older residents

ABOVE: The *Perth Gazette and Western Australian Journal* was first published on 5 January 1833. Coming into the hands of a number of owners and changing its name several times, it eventually became the *West Australian* in November 1879. Having become a daily newspaper in 1885, it established itself as a force to be reckoned with throughout the state and moved to a four-storey building on St Georges Terrace, east of William Street, known as West Australian Chambers. From here they moved to the newly constructed Newspaper House, also on St Georges Terrace, designed by architects Hobbs, Smith & Forbes. The building cost of £95,579 and opened during the centenary of the newspaper in 1933.

ABOVE: In November 1935 Newspaper House was awarded the Royal Institute of British Architects medal for the best street facade. For older Perth residents, the phrase, 'meet you at the clock' instantly conjures up a mental picture of the double-sided clock on the front of Newspaper House, which has been a popular meeting place for many years. The *West Australian* vacated the premises in 1988 and moved to Osborne Park. Newspaper House remained vacant for 20 years, until the plot behind was bought by BHP Billiton who constructed a 46-storey skyscraper between 2008 and 2012. Approval for the new office complex included strict conditions on maintaining the heritage value of the buildings along St Georges Terrace, which now form part of Brookfield Place, and are used as shops, offices and restaurants.

1861

PERTH BOYS' SCHOOL
The first custom-built school in Perth

ABOVE: In the first few years of the Swan River Colony, thoughts of educating the youngsters took second place to survival in a hostile environment. News of the lack of a school got back to England where the newspapers suggested Western Australia ran the risk of becoming a 'degraded society'. As a result, a colonial school was set up under the tutelage of John Cleland, a carpenter by trade, and for 17 years lessons of varying quality took place in temporary buildings around the town. An education committee was eventually convened and led to a school being built in St Georges Terrace, on the site of a mill. Designed by the Colonial Secretary, William Sandford, construction of the school started in 1853 using convict labour, but a shortage of materials delayed completion until 1854.

ABOVE: In common with most educational establishments of the time, the new school was built in the style of a church in order to imbue the pupils with a sense of duty, attentiveness and obedience. With two additional cross-wings, built in 1865 and 1867, the school continued in use until the 1890s, when it could no longer cater for a significant increase in population. A new school was built in James Street and the old one became the library for the new Perth Technical School. The impressive red-brick building on the left was built especially for the Technical School in 1910. In the mid-

1980s the college moved to other sites and the old Perth Boys' School was vested with the National Trust and leased as a café. In 2016 the use of this building turned full-circle and, conserved and restored, it has become a city-centre venue for Curtin University. Coincidentally, the old Technical School, which once offered classes in fine art, is now occupied by a busy art gallery. Both buildings are now part of the bustling Brookfield Place plaza – a far cry from the sleepy scene of 1861.

1862

BISHOP HALE'S SCHOOL / THE CLOISTERS

The first secondary school in Western Australia

ABOVE: The inaugural Anglican Bishop of Perth, Matthew Blagden Hale, had a keen interest in education and founded the first secondary school in Western Australia. After a fundraising campaign, which included a substantial personal donation from the bishop himself, a school building was designed by Richard Roach Jewell and built by convict labour on St Georges Terrace at Mill Street. Officially known as the Perth Church of England Collegiate School, it mainly attracted wealthy young men as pupils. The opening of the new school was reported in the *Inquirer* newspaper on 30 June 1858: 'The Bishop's School, Perth, was opened on Monday, when there was an attendance of about 23 scholars, a very good commencement.'

ABOVE: The building, which became known as the Cloisters, was enlarged and remodelled in 1879–80 and continued as a school until 1914. After this it was used by the Anglican Church as St John's University Hostel to provide accommodation for students at the newly formed University of Western Australia. In 1931 the building was damaged by fire and demolition was considered to make way for new buildings and a continuation of Mill Street. Instead, £2,000 was spent on its restoration, after which it had various uses, including as a WAAF barracks. Demolition was once again on the cards in the mid-1960s, but a campaign in the *West Australian* generated public support for its retention and it was eventually incorporated into a scheme for office buildings with a plaza and shopping arcade, which forms the building's backdrop today. Although the Cloisters stopped being used as a school over 100 years ago, Hale School is still up and running, now in Wembley Downs, making it the oldest private boys' school in Western Australia.

c. 1866

PENSIONER BARRACKS

The Tudor-style gatehouse arch is all that remains

ABOVE: The introduction of convicts in 1850 to augment the local labour force meant that people were also required to supervise and guard the prisoners. The Enrolled Pensioner Force, which was made up of retired British military personnel, travelled as guards on the convict ships arriving in Western Australia. On arrival, members of the force were offered a choice of 10 acres of land with which to make a living, or the opportunity to continue work as guards. For those who continued as guards, accommodation was required and so the Pensioner Barracks was designed by architect Richard Roach Jewell and constructed mainly by convict labour. The first families moved into their two-roomed apartments in 1866. Additional facilities for the barracks complex included a cook house, firing range and gun room, wash house, stores and stables and, later, a fives court. This photo shows the Enrolled Guards, as they later became known, standing in front of the nearly completed barracks.

ABOVE: The introduction of the Enrolled Pensioner Force only lasted for 18 years, but during that time some 2,500 guards and their families came to live in Western Australia. The force was disbanded in 1887 and the barracks were slowly converted into government offices. In 1960 the government announced that the barracks were to be demolished to make way for the Kwinana Freeway. This produced a public outcry and the Royal West Australian Historical Society formed the Barracks Defence Council to save the building. Despite this, demolition commenced and two bays of windows were reduced to rubble. Attention then turned to saving the gatehouse arch. After several polls to gauge public opinion, all of which were conclusively in favour of retention, a free vote was taken in parliament and a motion to demolish the arch was defeated by eight votes, leaving us with Perth's 'Arc de Triomphe' in front of Parliament House.

PERTH OBSERVATORY

Where standard time for Western Australia was first set

BELOW: The first Western Australian Government Astronomer, William Cooke, was appointed in 1896. His first task was to determine the exact latitude and longitude of Perth, while overseeing the construction of an observatory on Mount Eliza. Designed by architect George Temple-Poole, Perth Observatory was officially opened in 1900 by John Forrest, the first Premier of Western Australia. As well as accurate time keeping, the observatory was responsible for weather forecasting, navigation, astronomy and seismology. To facilitate this, three buildings were constructed: the Transit Circle Building, containing a meridian telescope; the Dome, which was a steel dome, similar to one at the Royal Observatory in Greenwich, used to take telescopic photographs of the night sky; and the Government Astronomer's office and family residence (seen on the right).

c. 1900

OBSERVATORY PERTH W.A.

BELOW: Having accurately calculated the coordinates of Perth, the Government Astronomer was able, for the first time in its history, to establish a standard time for Western Australia. From 1899 the correct time was displayed on a clock at the observatory gates. From November 1900 a signal was also sent electrically to a time-ball on Arthur Head, in Fremantle Harbour. The large ball dropped daily at 1 p.m. to enable ships' clocks to be accurately set. Because of excessive light pollution from the city, the observatory was dismantled in the early 1960s and moved to a new site in the Darling Ranges. The one remaining building on the old Perth Observatory site is the former chief astronomer's residence, now the headquarters of the National Trust of Western Australian.

1899

PERTH PARK / KINGS PARK
The largest inner-city park in the world

42

LEFT: This photo was taken from the tower of the Government Astronomer's house shortly after Kings Park had been landscaped. Known to the Whadjuk Noongar people as Mooro Katta and Kaarta Gar-up, Kings Park has always been a culturally important site. In 1832 Surveyor General to the Swan River Colony, John Septimus Roe, refused to allow timber to be felled on Mount Eliza (named after the wife of Governor Darling of New South Wales) as he intended it to be a public park. His edict was ignored, as the first export from the colony was 5 tonnes of jarrah, cut down within the park. Thankfully, in 1871 Roe's successor, Malcolm Fraser, persuaded Governor Weld to gazette 1.75 square kilometres (0.68 square miles) as public reserve, thus creating Perth's famous park. In 1890 the first Premier of Western Australia, Sir John Forrest, enlarged the park to its present size and it officially opened as Perth Park in August 1895.

ABOVE: In honour of the accession of King Edward VII in 1901, the park was renamed King's Park (the apostrophe was later dropped) during a visit by the Duke of Cornwall and Princess Mary. The trees planted in the last decade of the 19th century and the early years of the 20th, when the park was landscaped in a style typical of the era, now completely obscure the entrance, but the paths, pavilions and tea rooms for rest and recuperation and facilities to play games such as croquet, bowls and tennis are still present. At 4.06 square kilometres (1.57 square miles), it is the largest inner city park in the world, beating Central Park in New York by 0.64 square kilometres (0.25 square miles). More importantly, it is a place enjoyed by about 6 million visitors every year, who use the area, as it has been for thousands of years, as a source of beauty and relaxation.

1929

STATE WAR MEMORIAL
Honouring those who gave their lives for their country

ABOVE: One of the earliest memorials in Kings Park was originally known as the Fallen Soldiers' Memorial. Unveiled in 1902, it commemorated Western Australian soldiers killed in the Boer War. The Avenue of Honour was planted along May Drive in 1919 to remember those who fell in World War I. The centrepiece of the State War Memorial, overlooking Perth Water, is the Cenotaph. Unveiled on 24 November 1929, the 18-metre (59-foot) granite obelisk was designed by local architect and war hero, General Sir John Talbot Hobbs. Hobbs, who designed countless buildings in Western Australia and beyond, became renowned during World War I for his justice and integrity as a military leader.

ABOVE: The State War Memorial now consists of the Cenotaph, Court of Contemplation, Flame of Remembrance and Pool of Reflection, commemorating all Western Australians who have given their lives in the service of their country. Each year tens of thousands of people gather in Kings Park on Anzac Day (25 April) for a very moving dawn service to remember the fallen. The park also contains many other memorials, including the first state war memorial for the Aboriginal and Torres Strait Islander people from all three armed services who were killed in various conflicts around the world. A walk to the middle of the Botanic Gardens will bring you to the Pioneer Women's Memorial Fountain and the bronze Centenary of Western Australia Women's Suffrage Memorial.

c. 1910

LEAKE MEMORIAL, KINGS PARK
A monument for the third Premier of Western Australia

ABOVE: George Leake had two very short terms as Premier of Western Australia in 1901 and 1902, the second coming to an end when he died in office. The memorial was the result of a bequest from Leake's wife, who specifically requested a marble drinking fountain. Designed in Byzantine style by James Linton, the art instructor at the newly formed Perth Technical School, the fountain was unveiled in July 1904. The meandering paths and shade-giving trees around the fountain show how Kings Park had been landscaped as a pleasure ground. In the background can be seen the Perth Observatory buildings built on the slopes of Mount Eliza.

ABOVE: Today the area surrounding the Leake Memorial is one of the most heavily used parts of Kings Park. Just to the south of the memorial are the West Australian Botanic Gardens. This feature was moved here from Stirling Gardens in 1962 in order to better show off the flora of Western Australia to those visiting Perth for the British Empire and Commonwealth Games. Designed by John Oldham, the garden now houses examples of over half the state's 25,000 plant species, many of them unique to Western Australia. A recent addition to the collection is Gija Jumulu, a 36-tonne boab tree estimated to be around 750 years old, which was moved 3,200 kilometres (1,988 miles) from the Kimberley and planted in the Botanic Gardens in 2008. The photograph on the right shows an arbour leading to the Botanic Gardens.

MARKET GARDENS AT MOUNTS BAY ROAD

Artificial fertilizers and reliable irrigation brought about the demise of city-centre market gardening

BELOW: Perth's early settlers brought a variety of seeds for food crops, but they very soon discovered that the promise of a fertile river floodplain was completely false and that the soil was, in the words of novelist Anthony Trollope, 'eminently suitable for hour glasses'. Some fertile soil was found along the base of Mount Eliza and around the swamplands to the north of the town. These areas were soon put to use as fruit and vegetable gardens. With the introduction of convict labour in 1850, the population of Perth grew dramatically, which resulted in a large increase in those turning their hands to market gardening as a trade. Notable among these were Chinese immigrants, many of whom brought with them the knowledge and skills to be successful commercial gardeners. In this panoramic view over the Swan River, neat rows of vegetables can be seen at the foot of Mount Eliza along Mounts Bay Road.

1905

BELOW: Over one-third of the Chinese population of Western Australia was involved in the market garden industry and right up to the 1930s they were familiar figures in the older suburbs of Perth, pushing a cart and selling their wares on a regular delivery round. Slowly, the introduction of artificial fertilizers and reliable irrigation systems enabled areas of poorer soil outside the city to be turned into land suitable for horticulture. This brought about the decline and the ultimate demise of city-centre market gardening. Today the area which once supplied Perth with all manner of produce has been drastically re-profiled by the construction of the Kwinana Freeway and Narrows Bridge. Where potatoes and tomatoes once grew, commercial buildings, apartments and the Mount Hospital now stand. Opened in 1939 in St Georges Terrace, almost opposite the Barracks Arch, the hospital moved to its Mounts Bay Road location in 1986.

1929

MELBOURNE HOTEL

The heritage-listed hotel still graces the corner of Hay and Milligan Street

LEFT: The Melbourne Hotel, on the corner of Hay Street and Melbourne Road (now Milligan Street), was constructed for John de Baun in 1896 during the excitement of the gold rush. An influential entrepreneur from New Jersey, USA, de Baun came to Australia in the 1880s. After settling in Victoria, he moved to Broken Hill where he built his first hotel. Realising the opportunities the boom offered the hospitality industry, he followed the gold rush to Western Australia and set about developing a portfolio of hotels. The site of the Melbourne Hotel was originally occupied by the Eagle Tavern, which was purchased by de Baun from the Swan Brewery Company and demolished to make way for this handsome hotel.

ABOVE: In addition to its hotel trade, the Melbourne became a very popular city pub, until its ownership was transferred to a syndicate who converted it into a nightclub and cabaret lounge that operated throughout the 1980s under an assortment of names. In 1993 the building once again changed hands and was renovated with many of the internal fixtures, fittings and its cantilevered iron balcony (an unusual feature for Perth) being retained, keeping much of the character of this fine gold rush hotel. At the same time, a large extension, exactly matching the existing building, was built on the Hay Street frontage. The large pediment seen in the 1929 photograph was lost long before these renovations. At the time the above photograph was taken, the hotel was closed for major renovations and alterations. It reopened in 2018.

1974

PERTH ENTERTAINMENT CENTRE

Replaced by Perth Arena as part of the Perth City Links urban renewal project

ABOVE: Anyone in Perth who went to see David Bowie, AC/DC or Abba during the 1970s or 80s will remember the Perth Entertainment Centre. The brainchild of Brian Treasure of television station TVW-7 and theatrical entrepreneur Michael Edgley, this building was developed primarily to mount large stage and television shows in a custom-built venue. The construction was dogged with delays and interruptions, including strike action timed to coincide with key operations in the building process, which caused a budget overrun of $3 million. The complex, also containing a cinema, eventually opened as the Channel 7 Edgley Entertainment Centre in December 1974 with the Australian debut of the second *Disney on Parade* show.

ABOVE: With 8,000 seats, Perth Entertainment Centre was the city's largest entertainment venue and was listed in the *Guinness Book of World Records* as the largest purpose-built theatre containing a proscenium arch in the world. From its opening until 2002, it played host to a large range of events including musicals, circuses and even a Miss Universe contest. From 1990 until its closure, the centre was also home to the Perth Wildcats basketball team. When it closed there were initially plans for the venue to be redeveloped, but they never materialised. Eventually, Western Australia Government unveiled plans for a new arena to be built next to the old centre. The disused building was demolished in December 2011, to make way for the Perth City Link, reconnecting the city centre to Northbridge by means of sinking the Fremantle railway line. Its replacement, the Perth Arena, was opened in November 2012. The new entertainment and sporting arena has a full capacity of 15,000.

c. 1914

RUSSELL SQUARE
Modelled on London's fashionable fenced squares

ABOVE: Russell Square was set aside as a reserve in 1873 and given its name in honour of Lord John Russell, twice Prime Minister of Britain. It was set out to give the rapidly growing population in the area now known as Northbridge a public recreation space. Alterations to the park's design were made by Perth City Council in the mid-1880s and again in the late 1890s when its present design, based on the popular fenced squares of London, came into being. Because it was opposite the Italian community's favourite inn, the Victoria Hotel, it was a favourite spot for Italians to do their courting and became known as 'Parco dei Sospire' ('Park of Sighs'). In the middle-distance on the right-hand side of the photograph can be seen St Brigid's Catholic Church, which was dedicated in 1905.

ABOVE: The square has been re-landscaped on several occasions. One such improvement was the addition of a fountain, which, within days of being turned on, was vandalised. Newspaper reports reveal that the police eventually apprehended 'two grown up lads' for the crime. In 1994 Russell Square was upgraded by the installation of gateways, fencing, water features, lighting and a centrepiece rotunda. Another aspect of the refurbishment was the addition of 30 original sculptures, designed and constructed by local artists Greg James and Drago Dadich. In more recent times, the streets around the square have been redeveloped as apartments, bringing new life to the area. The park remains ever-popular as a place of recreation and has become one of the main centres for the very popular Perth Fringe Festival, which takes place every February.

c. 1897

GREAT WESTERN HOTEL
The remarkably well-preserved hostelry still graces the corner of William and James Streets

LEFT: After the Fremantle to Guildford railway line was completed and gold was discovered at Coolgardie, a large number of new buildings sprang up in the area centred on Perth Railway Station. Part of this rush of development was the Great Western Hotel. The hotel opened in November 1896 and received a glowing review in the *West Australian*, which was very complimentary about the lavish Federation Filigree design by local architect Michael Cavanagh. The cart on the right-hand side of the photograph belonged to Boan Bros., an emporium which Harry and Benjamin Boan had opened just over the railway line a year before the hotel. Boans became one of the best known department stores in Western Australia.

ABOVE: By the beginning of the 20th century, the Great Western Hotel had become one of the most popular hotels in Perth, probably because of its close proximity to the railway. An advertisement in the 1900 Christmas edition of the *Western Mail* drew attention to the convenient location and other attributes of the accommodation: 'It is most advantageously situated, being only one minute's walk from the Railway Station, and commanding one of the best views of the Metropolis. From the Spacious Promenade Balconies, with which each storey is furnished, can be discerned the blue waters of the Swan River.' Following a $1.5-million restoration in 1989, the hotel was renamed the Brass Monkey, after a beer brewed by the owners, and remains one of the most popular hotels in Perth.

1905

HORSESHOE BRIDGE

Perth's unique bridge continues to serve the same purpose today

ABOVE: When the Fremantle to Guildford railway line opened in 1880, a gated level-crossing was constructed at the line's intersection with William Street. Sixteen years later, for the convenience of pedestrians, a timber footbridge was added. As road and rail traffic in the burgeoning city increased, the level-crossing became a constant source of congestion and strong representation was made to the government for the crossing to be replaced with a bridge. Initially, a conventional bridge design was contemplated, but this was scrapped when it was realised how much would need to be paid in compensation to private land owners in the vicinity for its construction. To avoid this, a draughtsman in the Public Works Department, Robert Howard, designed a bridge in the shape of a horseshoe, thus minimising the encroachment on private property. Prominent on the horizon is the oldest section of the Western Australian Museum, behind the Perth Boys' School and Police Courts.

ABOVE: The bridge opened in 1904 and was immediately surrounded in controversy because of plans to demolish the footbridge. The main argument against this removal was that people would have to walk further to get across a semi-circular bridge. To appease passengers from the north of the city, a ticket office was set up on the bridge to save them having to walk round to the front of the building. With few other bridges of this shape in the world, the Horseshoe Bridge has remained a unique feature of Perth's transport system and still serves its purpose very well. In 2009 the bridge underwent major renovation and conservation work and was closed for seven months. With its pedestal lamps in the form of a swan at each end, the bridge now forms an unusual backdrop to the eastern end of Yagan Square, one of the city's newest piazzas.

RIGHT: Taken in 2014, this elevated shot of Horseshoe Bridge shows the recently excavated tunnel conveying the railway lines underground to create the new City Link between the city centre and Northbridge.

2014

CITY MARKETS

The old market site is now at the heart of Perth's City Link redevelopment

BELOW: In 1852 the government reported that there was no suitable land available for a market, 'the lack of which was felt as a serious grievance by the inhabitants of Perth'. A market was established on the Town Hall Undercroft in 1872, but it closed within five years. Over the next 20 years various overtures were made towards developing a new market, but it wasn't until 1892 that the question was raised in earnest and the government offered the city council a loan of £5,000 to establish a market. Eventually, however, it was the government who erected a market building on the corner of William and Wellington Streets to the delight of all. The advertising hoarding to the right of the market building masks the water tower for Perth Railway Station.

BELOW: After World War I, another market further west on Wellington Street was opened to promote direct trade between producers and consumers. Initially a great success, its business slowly declined and the market closed in 1934. The Department of Agricultural took over the market building in 1936 and leased a small section to the council for a fish market. One year later, the building was demolished to enable the widening of Wellington Street. During the course of demolition, one contractor fell to his death from the roof. The site was eventually used in 1973 for the Perth Central Bus Station, which in turn was demolished in 2014 to make way for Yagan Square as part of Perth City Link. This urban renewal project reconnects the central business district with Northbridge by putting the railway underground and creating a new mixed-use precinct. Although almost everything has altered since the 1935 photograph, the view is still framed by the posts of the Horseshoe Bridge on the right and the elaborate verandah of the Royal Hotel (established in 1882) on the left.

1870

WESLEY CHURCH

A continuous place of worship since 1870

LEFT: A block of land on the corner of Hay and William Streets was purchased in 1867 by the Methodist congregation of Perth in order to build a new church for their growing flock. To encourage public donations for the new church, a pew incentive scheme was developed, by which the best seats in the church were allocated to those who donated the most money. George Shenton (later the first Mayor of Perth) and Joseph Hardey (a farmer and Wesleyan layman) would have been in the front row, as between them they donated half the required funds. The church was designed by Richard Roach Jewell and completed shortly before this photograph was taken in 1870.

ABOVE: In 1875 Wesley Church became the proud owner of the first pipe organ in Western Australia. Some 20 years later, to accommodate an ever-increasing congregation, galleries were constructed on each side of the nave. More recently the church has undergone two major restoration projects, one to repair the damage from the Meckering Earthquake of 1968, with a further $150,000 being spent 20 years later to restore external walls, gables, parapets and the tower. The church also redeveloped some of its land around the north and west sides of the church with the construction of the Wesley Arcade and Tower (behind), which opened in May 1976. In relatively recent times, the corner outside the church has become a well-known Sunday afternoon speakers' corner, where the problems of the world are given a lively airing.

1926

HIS MAJESTY'S THEATRE

The most majestic theatre building in Western Australia

LEFT: The plot on which His Majesty's Theatre sits had been a popular entertainment venue for fairs and outdoor theatre since the 1870s. In 1902 Thomas Malloy, one of the wealthiest men in Perth, acquired the plot in order to give Perth its second theatre since the Theatre Royal opened in 1897. His Majesty's Theatre was designed by architect William Wolf who immigrated to Australia in 1877. He worked in Sydney and Melbourne before setting up practice in Perth in the mid-1890s. Costing £46,000 and taking around two years to complete, the building was constructed by Gustav Liebe, who also built the Melbourne Hotel. The opening of the theatre in 1904 was postponed several times before taking place on Christmas Eve. Even then, the lock on the main gates jammed and workmen had to prize the gates open before anyone could get in.

ABOVE: The auditorium featured four artificial waterfalls, reputed to improve ventilation, which disappeared early in the life of the theatre, probably because they gave those in the front few rows of the stalls an unexpected shower every now and then. Additional ventilation was provided on hot evenings by a retractable dome in the ceiling. The theatre is believed to be the only remaining working Edwardian theatre in Australia and is one of only two His Majesty's theatres in the world (the other being in Aberdeen, Scotland). Sadly, the original facade was altered significantly in World War II, when the original balconies were demolished in order to conform to a local government byelaw. The building was nearly demolished in 1971, but local supporters mounted a successful campaign for its retention and it was extensively renovated in the late 1970s. Today it remains an extremely popular performing arts venue.

1899

HAY STREET TRAMLINE CONSTRUCTION
Trams served the city and its suburbs from 1899 to 1958

ABOVE: The first gold rush brought a huge population explosion to Perth which necessitated the creation of new suburbs. As a result, the need for a cheap, reliable public transport system became an imperative. During the last half of the 1890s a number of newspaper correspondents suggested that a tram system would fill the need. After much debate about the initial route, Hay Street was decided upon and the work of laying the tram lines commenced at the end of January 1899. By early July of that year, the *Kalgoorlie Miner* was able to announce that the first test run of a tram had taken place and the line would be open in a couple of months. The spires of Wesley Church and the Town Hall can be seen in the distance.

ABOVE: The opening of the first tram service in Perth, operated by Perth Electric Tramways Ltd., took place on 28 September 1899. A report the following day in the *West Australian* suggests it caused quite a stir: 'The principal event in the city yesterday was undoubtedly the opening of the Hay Street tram cars to traffic.' As the city grew, so did the tram system, which weaved its way through a number of suburbs. After World War II the system was considered old-fashioned, so was replaced by trolley-buses, with the last tram running in 1958. Today, while there has been much debate about the reinstatement of a tram service, the city centre's fare-free public transport system includes CAT buses, which operate on four routes around the central business district. The spires of Wesley Church and the Town Hall are now obscured by other buildings, but the elegant Art Deco lines of the Gledden Building tower are visible on the right.

c. 1975

PICCADILLY ARCADE

The cinema may have gone but the Art Deco arcade is now heritage listed

LEFT: At the time of the Great Depression in the 1930s, going to the cinema became a popular escape from the harsh realities of life. One of the many cinemas to be constructed around Perth at this time was the Piccadilly. Part of the Piccadilly Arcade, which ran between Hay and Murray Streets, this theatre was built for the flamboyant Claude de Bernales, a local mining entrepreneur and businessman. The Art Deco arcade opened in February 1938 and was described at the time as 'strikingly designed'. The cinema opened a month later with a charity gala screening of Claudette Colbert's film, *I Met Him in Paris*. This photograph was taken at a time when Murray Street was still open to two-way traffic.

BELOW: A crowded Piccadilly Arcade in 1951.

1951

ABOVE: When built, the Piccadilly Theatre reflected the optimism and desire for enjoyable entertainment that characterised the end of the Great Depression. Although the theatre and arcade underwent a major refurbishment in 1984, many of the sumptuous decorative elements, such as friezes of dancing girls moulded by Perth sculptor Edward Kohler, can still be seen. Sadly, with fierce competition from the multi-screen cinemas in Perth's suburbs, the Piccadilly, the last working cinema in the city centre, turned off the projector one final time in 2013, leaving the ghost of a former manager, who fell to his death down the stairs one night, in peace and quiet. This spectre is said to have been first seen by a workman, who claimed a 'shadowy figure' walked across the foyer to the lift while he was working in the building. No longer open to two-way traffic, Murray Street is now part of a pedestrianised shopping area.

RIGHT: The Piccadilly Arcade is still a popular shopping mall, but now sadly bereft of its cinema.

1937

LONDON COURT

The Tudor-style arcade has become a major tourist attraction

ABOVE: London Court was built during a period when most West Australians prided themselves on being 'British'. The site for the arcade, originally known as Gun Alley, was purchased by Claude de Bernales, who conceived it to be part of a thoroughfare connecting Perth Railway Station to the Esplanade. Work started on the construction in August 1936. When completed, almost a year later, it was revealed as a half-timbered arcade in imitation Tudor style with huge wrought-iron gates at each end, featuring hand carvings, gargoyles, masks, shields and crests. The opening of London Court, shown in this photo from 1937, was celebrated with a three-day charity, 'Ye Olde English Fayre', which raised £2,000 for the new Perth Hospital.

ABOVE: At the time of opening, the flats above the shops in the arcade were considered to be ultra-modern, all having air-conditioning (the first in the state with this luxury), fitted kitchens and bathrooms, plus, as one sale brochure explained, 'provision has been made for the installation of a telephone'. Today they have mainly been converted into commercial premises, reflecting a Perth trend from the recent past for suburban rather than city-centre living. Loved by some and hated by others, London Court is an anachronism which has become a major tourist attraction. The automaton depictions of a jousting tournament and the fight between St George and the Dragon, above the clocks at each end of the arcade, never fail to draw a crowd.

1922

CENTRAL ARCADE / FORREST PLACE

Central Arcade was demolished just 16 years after it opened

ABOVE: Due to its hot, sunny climate, covered malls have been a popular feature of shopping in central Perth since the first one, the Busy Bee Arcade, opened in 1894 on William Street. Central Arcade, which ran from Wellington Street (opposite Perth Railway Station) to Murray Street, was opened in 1906. The building was a tall, barn-like construction, clad in corrugated iron, with glass skylights along the apex of the roof. Initially, instead of individual, self-contained retail units, the building was divided into stalls, stable-like, from which each trader operated. With the stalls eventually replaced by shop fronts, the arcade thrived until the outbreak of World War I. This photo shows the demolition of Central Arcade with the nearly completed General Post Office on the left.

RIGHT: The interior of Central Arcade, just a couple of years before its demolition.

c. 1920

ABOVE: Central Arcade was demolished in 1922 to improve the surroundings of the new General Post Office building and to make way for a new street. The GPO and the new street, Forrest Place, opened in 1923. Opposite the GPO, the Padbury Buildings were built

and opened in 1925. Original plans for this building were for a grand three-storey structure, but this was reduced by one level in the final design. During the construction, a tragic accident occurred when a construction crane toppled over, killing its driver.

In 1986 it was decided to turn Forrest Place into a pedestrian precinct and demolish the Padbury Building and Boans' Department Store to create Forrest Chase Shopping Centre. The new complex was officially opened by Queen Elizabeth II in 1988.

c. 1930

74

GENERAL POST OFFICE BUILDING
Architectural elegance and grandeur in Forrest Place

LEFT: Land opposite the railway station, including Central Arcade (see previous spread), was acquired by the Commonwealth Government in 1911 to create a precinct to which government departments could move from the cramped Treasury Building at the corner of St Georges Terrace and Barrack Street. The proposal was for a new street (Forrest Place) through the site, on which a General Post Office would be built. Eventually, groundwork for the Beaux-Arts-style GPO building commenced in July 1914, with the foundation stone being laid the following year. War intervened, however, and construction ground to a halt. After the war, the project was further delayed by several changes to the design, eventually opening in September 1923. The Central Hotel, on the corner of Wellington Street, first appears in the street directory in 1909.

ABOVE: In 1933 the Commonwealth Government precinct was enlarged by the addition of the Commonwealth Bank, south of the GPO. Designed in a similar style to its neighbour, it makes an elegant compatriot in an area dominated by modern buildings. Forrest Place was closed to traffic in 1987 to create a pedestrian mall with the GPO building as its backdrop. In recent years the mall has been refurbished with the addition of a children's water play feature, stage area and a distinctive sculpture, 'the Cactus', at the northern end. Forrest Place, which has long been a favoured venue for protests and rallies, continues to be a community focal point of the city in which Friday night hawkers' markets have become a very popular attraction. Central Hotel was demolished and replaced with Albert Facey House in 1989. The 52-storey Bankwest Tower on the left at 108 St Georges Terrace is currently occupied by South32, a base metal and coal mining company.

1881

PERTH RAILWAY STATION
A modest station serving Perth's first passenger railway service

ABOVE: After much debate about the need and route, the Fremantle to Guildford railway was constructed and the first train ran on a 3-kilometre (1.9-mile) section of track from Fremantle to North Fremantle in August 1880. In March the following year the line was opened to Guildford, later being extended to Midland Junction and on to Northam. One of the principal stations on the line was that in central Perth and

designs for the building in Neoclassical style were drawn up by architect George Temple-Poole. The building had one through platform (the line was initially run on a single track) and two terminating bay platforms, one at each end of the station. Within a very short space of time both passenger and goods traffic on the line exceeded all expectations. Just visible behind the station is the top of the 1856 Perth Gaol.

ABOVE: With the formation of the Western Australian Government Railways to run the new rail system, administrative offices were required and a second storey was added to Perth Railway Station, which remained the department's headquarters until it was disbanded in 2003. A planned third storey with an imposing clock tower was never built, but a number of station buildings have been added to the complex over the years. The Fremantle to Midland line was closed in September 1979, but, following public outcry and a vigorous campaign, the line reopened in 1983. As part of the enlargement of the metropolitan rail network, the station was refurbished and two new underground platforms, built at 90 degrees to the existing ones, were opened in 2007. Today Perth Railway Station is an important transport hub serving many hundreds of thousands of commuters every year.

1905

PERTH BOYS' AND GIRLS' SCHOOL / PICA

The heritage building is now at the heart of Perth Cultural Centre

ABOVE: Enrolments in the boys' school on St Georges Terrace grew so much in the 1880s and 90s that the building was unable to accommodate them all. To address this, construction of a new school building started in 1895. Two years later, Perth Boys' and Girls' School in James Street, north of the railway line, was officially opened by the Minister for Education, Edward Wittenoom. The new building, which accommodated 500 boys on the ground floor and 500 girls on the upper, was the largest project undertaken by the Education Department in that era. At the time of opening, the girls and boys each had separate entrances to the school. In 1900 two additional classrooms were added, each designed to house a further 75 children.

ABOVE: In 1936 a new girls' school opened in East Perth and the entire James Street complex was given over to the boys' school, which, 11 years later, was renamed Perth Boys' High School. During the 1950s, residential development in the inner city decreased and the growth of the suburbs displaced inner city living. The school closed in 1958 and the building was used by Perth Technical College until 1988. Now the home of Perth Institute of Contemporary Arts (PICA), the old school has a number of defined spaces including a café, performance space, gallery and administrative offices. PICA is situated right in the middle of the Perth Cultural Centre, which is home to a number of cultural institutions such as the Art Gallery of Western Australia, Western Australian Museum, State Library of Western Australia and the State Theatre Centre.

c. 1903

WESTERN AUSTRALIAN MUSEUM
The state's premier museum is still expanding its impressive collection

1929

OPPOSITE: Originally established in 1891 as a geological museum with a collection of specimens housed in the Old Perth Gaol building, the Western Australian Museum, as it became known, moved into the Byzantine-style Jubilee Building shown here in 1897. The original plan was to have a combined library, museum and art gallery on St Georges Terrace as a commemoration of Queen Victoria's Golden Jubilee, but enthusiasm for the project died and it was abandoned in 1894. After a great deal of procrastination, the government selected a site on the corner of James and Beaufort Streets and the museum project eventually reached fruition in 1897. In the new building, the collection was extended to include ethnological and natural history sections.

LEFT: Static exhibits on display in Hackett Hall, a far cry from today's dynamic museum visitor experience.

ABOVE: The first years of the 20th century saw a flurry of building activity on the museum site. The Government Geology Building was completed in 1902 and, a year later, the Victoria Library was built to make space in the Jubilee Building for the ever-growing collection. Five years later, the art gallery wing on Beaufort Street was added and in 1913 the magnificent Hackett Hall was completed as an extension to the library. A seven-storey brutalist building was added in 1973, with a later glass foyer providing a modern link between the Jubilee Wing and Hackett Hall. In 2016 the museum closed for four years so that a large new building could be constructed on the northern side of the present buildings to provide Western Australia with a world-class 21st-century museum.

c. 1914

SWAN BARRACKS

The fortress-like entrance now welcomes backpackers

ABOVE: An 1896 report by the Commandant for the Local Forces of Western Australia expressed concern that local Volunteer Corps in the state were not sufficiently well organised, trained or disciplined for war. The report concluded that competent instruction in good drill halls would significantly improve this. As a result, Swan Barracks was built the same year as one of these drill halls. The location was considered central enough for use by the Perth Company of WA Rifle Volunteers, who shared the space with school cadets. A fortress-like stone building with portcullis, designed by George Temple-Poole, was added in 1897. This striking Francis Street entrance to the barracks was built to provide space for administrative offices. This photograph shows men enlisting at the Swan Barracks during World War I.

ABOVE: At the beginning of the 20th century, the Swan Barracks gained a number of additional buildings and a third storey to the administrative offices. Following Federation on 1 January 1901, the barracks were incorporated into the Australian Army and became the Fifth Military District Headquarters, which played a significant role during World War I as a recruitment and training centre. During the first years of World War II, further enlargement took place and a new wing was added on the west side in the mid-1950s. Throughout these alterations, George Temple-Poole's citadel-like building remained a focal point, as it does today. The army vacated the barracks in 1992 and moved to the old HMAS *Leeuwin* site in Fremantle. Eventually the barracks site was sold in 1999 and is now a popular city-centre backpackers' hostel.

TRADES HALL

A powerhouse for the Trades Union movement in Western Australia

1930

LEFT: Perth's Trades and Labour Council, which was formed in 1891, regrouped in 1907 as the Western Australian Branch of the Australian Labour Federation. From this, a Metropolitan District Council was formed to represent the interests of the union organisations in Perth. This body first met in 1910 at the Shearer Memorial Hall in Beaufort Street, for which they had secured a lease from the Presbyterian Church. A year later, the Perth Trades Hall Association was established and was soon in negotiation with the church over the outright purchase of the land. After much hard work to secure funds, the foundation stone of a new Trades Hall was laid in 1911 by the Labour Prime Minister Andrew Fisher and a year later the front portion of the Trades Hall at 80 Beaufort Street opened. In 1923 the Unity Theatre was added at the back of the building and was used for official Trade Union functions, as well as theatre productions, dancing and boxing matches.

BELOW: Further additions were made to the building in 1934, including a large hall, built to accommodate 2,000 people. The Unity Theatre was converted into offices in 1966, and in 1973 the 1934 building was completely demolished to make way for a multi-storey office building named Curtin House (shown on the left in this photo), which is currently used as a police station. After a number of other alterations, the Trades and Labour Council sold the building in 1985 to an art gallery and moved to newer, more versatile premises in Brewer Street. Eighteen years later, the building returned to its original use when the Construction, Forestry, Mining and Energy Union purchased it and began a significant renovation project to return it, as far as possible, to its original design. In 2014 the building reopened and was winner of a State Heritage Award for its conservation and adaptive reuse.

1885

BARRACK STREET BRIDGE
The rebuilt bridge helped to improve the alignment of Barrack and Beaufort Streets

ABOVE: Looking south across the second Barrack Street Bridge.

OPPOSITE: To carry Beaufort Street across the new Guildford to Fremantle railway line, a timber bridge (centre left) was constructed in 1880, but the bridge was found to be too narrow and in constant need of repair from very early on in its life. After protracted negotiations between the city council and government, a new, more substantial bridge was built in 1894. The construction of this bridge offered an ideal opportunity to improve the alignment of Barrack and Beaufort Streets, which had a very awkward dog-leg, much hated by cab and other commercial drivers. By pulling down the Working Men's Institute (centre), on the junction between Barrack and Wellington Streets, a much safer junction was created to the satisfaction of all. This picture from 1885 is looking north from the Town Hall on Barrack Street towards Beaufort Street. The large building on the upper-left-hand side is the Old Perth Gaol of 1856.

ABOVE: With a heavy increase in traffic, the second Barrack Street Bridge also became obsolete soon after its construction; it was too narrow and not substantial enough to carry the load imposed by the traffic flow in a rapidly growing Perth. In 1903, consideration was given to building a horseshoe bridge, like the one built across William Street, but this was rejected on the grounds that its shape was inconvenient for traffic. Soon after, the existing bridge was demolished and an even bigger and stronger one built in its place in 1908. A much grander affair than its predecessors, this bridge, using Donneybrook stone and Meckering granite for its features, included cast-iron light poles. Although altered several times since, the current bridge retains many of its original 1908 features. The Old Perth Gaol building still exists but was subsumed by the Western Australian Museum (centre top) in 1891.

1901

BARRACK STREET

This ethnically diverse street was a major thoroughfare for trams

ABOVE: In the early 1900s Barrack Street appeared to be a sea of telephone lines. The introduction of a telephone system in 1887 brought with it a plethora of wires strung on poles down every main street in central Perth, all leading to a small manual telephone exchange in Wellington Street. Additionally, the street became one of the main thoroughfares for the trams going from a terminus on Barrack Square to the newly created suburbs of North Perth and Mount Lawley. With the convenience of the trams, Barrack Street became an important retail centre with an ethnically diverse

array of shops, including a Chinese grocer, Greek fishmonger, German butcher and the Irish-run Railway Hotel, all serving the newly developed northern suburbs. As with most views of Barrack Street, the tower of the Town Hall is the focal point of this photo. The tall building, now known as the Bon Marche Arcade, on the left near the Town Hall, was built by W.G. Brookman, who, as the banners on the left show, was campaigning to become mayor at the time this photograph was taken.

ABOVE: Taking the telephone wires underground helped to increase Barrack Street's popularity as a shopping precinct, with a popular addition to the retail outlets being the Bon Marche Arcade (the cream-coloured stucco building in front of the Town Hall), which opened in 1901. Perth radio station 6PR also started its life on Barrack Street in 1931, broadcasting from a studio above Nicholson's Music Centre (just beyond the blue-roofed building) until it moved to new studios in Hay Street after World War II.

Another source of entertainment on the street was the 450-seat Liberty Theatre in a converted first floor office, which became renowned in the 1950s for screening Italian and French 'art films'. The street is still dominated by the majestic Town Hall building and remains home to many small businesses, cafés and restaurants. On the right-hand corner can be seen the Stockade Building, an exuberant example of 1910 Perth architecture.

1885

TWISS STREET (HAY STREET)

The tip of Wesley Church's spire is the only thing still visible in this view looking west from the Town Hall

LEFT: In the early days, Perth streets seem to have been named to ingratiate British politicians. Originally Hay Street had two names: from the Town Hall eastwards it was called Howick Street, after Viscount Howick, Prime Minister of England (1830–34); while the western end was named Twiss Street, after Horace Twiss, Under-Secretary of State for War and the Colonies (1828–30). In 1897 the entire length of the street was renamed Hay Street after Robert William Hay, who was yet another Permanent Under-Secretary of State for the Colonies (1825–36). To the right of Wesley Church, on William Street, can be seen the previous Methodist Church, with its small belfry perched on the roof.

RIGHT: Like St Georges Terrace, Hay Street underwent huge changes during the first gold rush. It became one of the city's principal shopping streets, with a wide variety of businesses flourishing thanks to the significant increase in population the rush brought with it. Prior to this time, the western end was primarily workers' cottages with shops, coal yards, smithies and foundries, but in the mid-1890s smaller businesses began to establish themselves in existing cottages and a number of larger enterprises erected substantial new offices and warehouses in the area. Now dominated by the city's multi-storey buildings, the tip of the spire of Wesley Church (barely visible in this view) is the only thing to have survived the many redevelopments Hay Street has undergone since the 1885 photograph. The prominent skyscrapers in this view are the 214-metre (702-foot) 108 St Georges Terrace (currently occupied by South32) and Perth's tallest building, the 226-metre (741-foot) Central Park (currently occupied by Rio Tinto).

1929

THEATRE ROYAL AND HOTEL METROPOLE
Custom-built luxury on Hay Street

LEFT: The Theatre Royal was Perth's first custom-built theatre and the brain-child of Perth politician and property developer Thomas Malloy. The Hotel Metropole, which opened in 1894, was constructed first and considered to be the most luxurious hotel in Perth. The hotel occupied the right-hand side of this grand building designed in Federation Free Classical style. Once the hotel opened, plans were made for a 1,000-seat theatre next door. The foundation stone for the theatre was laid in May 1895 and when completed it included all mod-cons, such as a sliding roof in the auditorium dome and Tobin air shafts to provide ventilation 'without draughts' on hot nights. The theatre should have opened on 17 April 1897, but it was delayed by two days because the SS *Rockton*, which was transporting the actors and scenery, was caught in a storm.

RIGHT: By the middle of World War I, the Theatre Royal had been upstaged by the larger His Majesty's Theatre (also built by Malloy), further west on Hay Street. The Royal started to show films and continued with a mixed program of film and variety acts until 1934, when the lease was purchased by Perth cinema pioneer James Stiles. From then on no live acts appeared in the theatre, which focused instead on mainstream films from the major distributors of the day. The hotel was converted into a shop in 1963, with the guest accommodation transformed into storage areas. Like so many theatres and cinemas around the world in the 1970s, the Royal suffered at the hands of television and ever-dwindling audiences. The theatre screened its last film on 9 February 1978. After this the ground floor was converted into shops, with the upstairs rooms and auditorium left empty.

AMBASSADORS THEATRE

Perth's Hollywood-inspired picture palace

BELOW: The 2,000-seater Ambassadors Theatre was probably the most extravagant cinema building Perth has ever seen. It was built in 1928 following a visit to America by the Head of Union Cinemas, Stuart Doyle, who came back besotted with the fashionable 'atmospheric' cinemas he had seen in places like San Francisco and Los Angeles. Union's architect, Henry White, adapted the American cinema style and the company proceeded to build cinemas to an 'atmospheric' design in Sydney and Perth. The idea of this design was to transport the patron to an exotic European courtyard, in which the audience would be comfortable residents in another time and place. The theatre opened in September 1929 and immediately wooed its audience with its house orchestra and the largest Wurlitzer pipe organ in Australia.

1929

1929

BELOW: Not long after the theatre opened, the Wall Street Crash plunged the world into a deep recession and the Ambassadors was hit by dwindling audiences. The orchestra was dismissed and the theatre closed for some months in late 1932, reopening the following year under new management. Another change of management in 1937 heralded a radical redesign of the building, removing as much of the 'atmospheric'

LEFT: The alluring interior of the Ambassadors Theatre at the time of its opening.

decoration as possible and remodelling both the interior and exterior in an Art Deco style. The theatre continued as a popular venue throughout World War II and in 1953 became the first cinema in Western Australia to show a film in Cinemascope. The Ambassadors closed on 4 February 1972 and was demolished soon afterwards to make way for a retail shopping complex.

1870

PERTH TOWN HALL
The clock tower at the corner of Barrack and Hay Streets is Perth's most famous landmark

LEFT: In 1866 Governor John Hampton announced the construction of Perth Town Hall as part of a program of public works being undertaken by convict labour. The building was designed by the Supervisor of Public Works, Richard Roach Jewell, who based his Victorian Free Gothic design on the medieval town halls of Europe. Construction of the building started the following year and was expected to take 12 months to complete. Instead, it took three years, during which time the labouring convicts were thought to have added the arrow-shaped windows on the tower and decorative motifs resembling a hangman's rope. The official opening took place on Foundation Day, 1 June, 1870, when Governor Weld formally handed over responsibility for the building to the City Council.

BELOW: McNess's ironmongers shop (also visible on the right of the main photo) sold everything from fishing nets to oil lamps and much of the equipment required by prospectors off to Coolgardie in search of gold.

c. 1886

RIGHT: A daily market was opened in the undercroft of the Town Hall 1872, but it did not last very long as the space was felt too gloomy for a market and was put to other uses. In 1875 explorer Ernest Giles arrived in Perth following his expedition from South Australia. His camels were stabled in the undercroft while the city hosted a welcoming party upstairs. The council's first fire engine was also kept in the undercroft, but the cost of horses to pull it proved too expensive, so those from the cab rank outside were borrowed to pull the engine to a fire. Eventually the Town Hall's ground-level arches were filled in to create shops and offices, which remained until the building's restoration in 2005. On several occasions plans to redevelop the building have been suggested, but none have come to fruition and the Town Hall remains very dear to the heart of Perth's citizens. McNess's ironmongers shop, on the opposite corner of Hay and Barrack Streets, was replaced by McNess Royal Arcade in 1897. This fine building (which can be seen on the right) was Perth's first city-centre shopping arcade and remained so until it was converted into shops in the 1980s. In 2014 the facade was conserved and renovated, but at the time of writing both upper floors remain unoccupied.

1906

BARRACK STREET LOOKING SOUTH FROM THE TOWN HALL

A number of 19th-century buildings have survived the widespread redevelopment

LEFT: Barrack Street was initially developed with housing for soldiers and officers as well as merchants' homes, warehouses and businesses. The Swan River end of Barrack Street was an important terminus for river transport and the site of a jetty from Perth's foundation. The first jetty was built by Henry Cole in 1829 and, for many years, was known as Cole's Jetty before being renamed Barrack Street Jetty. To cater for the increase in river transport and recreational needs brought about by the huge influx of people to Perth in the 1890s, several further jetties were built in conjunction with Barrack Square, which was completed in 1906 and designed to resemble a Union Jack. The onion-domed City Baths can be seen centre right and an embryonic South Perth stretches out beyond. The tall turreted building is T&G Chambers, built for the Temperance & General Life Assurance Company in 1897.

RIGHT: A large increase in the popularity of river trips came with the opening of Barrack Square, from which excursion steamers now ran instead of from William Street Jetty. Since its initial construction, the square has undergone a number of changes in design, but the most major change came in 1998, when the jetties and square underwent major redevelopment, including a new ferry terminal. Centrepiece of the new-look square was the construction of Perth's iconic Bell Tower (seen at the end of Barrack Street) in 2000. Also known as Swan Bells or the Swan Tower, the glass and copper structure contains over 50 bells and is open to the public daily. It is unique in being the only bell tower in the world designed to showcase the English art of change ringing. Thankfully, the Central Government Offices and the Weld Club have survived since the 1906 photograph to provide an excellent cross-section of the history of this street. T&G Chambers was demolished and replaced by Citibank House in 1962.

c. 1879

CENTRAL GOVERNMENT OFFICES

An architecturally significant block of 19th-century buildings

ABOVE: Incorporating part of the old Barracks Guard House, the collection of interlinking buildings along Barrack Street reflect the 19th-century practice of placing government departments in one location. The first section of what would come to be known as the Central Government Offices was built in 1874. Containing law courts and a Land Registry, it was designed by Richard Roach Jewell. Three years later, tenders were invited for the completion of the Barrack Street facade down to St Georges Terrace. The Director of Public Works described the new offices as 'having free circulation of air and commodious chambers in a building where a number of Public Officers and others are employed for many hours a day'. The commodious chambers are shown here looking down Barrack Street towards the Town Hall.

RIGHT: Central Government Offices extension on St Georges Terrace.

1889

ABOVE: The next section to be constructed was the eastern wing, on the corner of Cathedral Avenue, which was completed in 1884. Two years later, the infill between this and the Barrack Street building was commenced, containing a Post Hall and Telegraph Office. Construction of this section was hampered when it was discovered that earlier work had been built on very poor foundations. A third storey was added during the 1890s to a design by George Temple-Poole, which gave the building a very French appearance. Finally, the crowning glory of the group, the Titles Office, at the northern end of Cathedral Avenue, was completed in 1897. The building continued in government use until 1996 when it was vacated. After a long period of disuse, the building has been given a new lease of life as a hotel and public plaza.

1905

ST GEORGE'S CHAMBERS
Cathedral Square is seen as the historic heart of Perth

LEFT: A policeman stands in front of the Central Government Offices, with St George's Chambers on the right and the west-end of St George's Cathedral on the far right. At the furthest end of Cathedral Avenue can be seen the Bon Marche drapery store (formerly Cargeeg Dimant & Co) on Hay Street. The first building on the site where St George's Chambers stood was the old St George's Cathedral. This building was opened as St George's Church in January 1845 and was elevated to the status of cathedral when the Anglican Diocese of Perth was formed in 1858. With the construction of a new cathedral 30 years later, the old church was demolished in 1891 and replaced by St George's Chambers, which housed the diocesan offices and a number of businesses.

ABOVE: St George's Chambers remained until the late 1970s when it was demolished to make way for a new Law Chambers building, which opened in 1981. Once heralded as Perth's 'ugliest modern building', it was partly demolished in 2012 as part of the Cathedral Square redevelopment and has since been replaced by a new Perth City Library building. Designed by local architect Kerry Hill, the seven-storey, purpose-built library is the first major civic building since the construction of the Perth Concert Hall over 40 years ago. The new library, with its stone-clad columns, is a striking addition to the classical and Gothic architecture of the old Centre Government Offices and St George's Cathedral. The Cathedral Square redevelopment has transformed the area into a vibrant focal point for community events and activities.

ST GEORGE'S CATHEDRAL

The tower was eventually added in 1902

BELOW: Despite Bishop Hale's protestations that 'there was neither sufficient money nor resources of other kinds' for the construction of a new cathedral in Perth, impetus was given to the project when Hale resigned in 1875. Four years later, work began on the present cathedral, which was designed by Sydney architect Edmund Blackett. The foundation stone was laid by the Governor, Sir William Robinson, in November 1880. The new building, which was positioned to the south and west of the old cathedral, was built of bricks made from clay dug in what is now called Queen's Gardens, with stone for trimmings quarried at Rottnest Island. The cathedral was consecrated in 1888, but funds were not sufficient to complete Blackett's design and his graceful tower and spire were omitted. St George's Chambers, which housed the diocesan offices, is on the left.

c. 1895

ANGLICAN CATHEDRAL PERTH. W. A.
A. PICKERING. PHOTO-PERTH. W. A.

BELOW: A revised design for the cathedral's tower was eventually completed in 1902, with its ring of eight bells being cast as a memorial to Queen Victoria. The Soldiers' Memorial Chapel, which took the place of the Chapter House in the original designs, was added in 1923 in memory of Anglican members of the AIF from Western Australia who fought in World War I. The cathedral also has a wooden cross, which originally marked the graves of WA soldiers killed during battle, and was rescued from a burning church at Villers-Bretonneux in northern France. An extensive restoration of the cathedral, including a new slate roof and stabilisation of the tower structure, took place in 2005–2008. Outside the cathedral, an eye-catching sculpture, *Ascalon*, captures the battle of St George and the Dragon in abstract form and was officially unveiled in 2011. Perth City Library, which was completed in 2016, sits on the site of the old St George's Chambers building.

1861

GOVERNMENT HOUSE
Old Government House was an undesirable residence

ABOVE: After initially living under canvas, Governor Stirling moved into a temporary wooden building while plans were made for the first permanent vice-regal residence. After a great many problems, both political and structural, the building, designed by Perth's chief civil engineer Henry Reveley, was completed in 1837. It was described by one commentator as having 'more the appearance of a lunatic asylum than the residence of the representative of the Queen'. Aesthetic quality, however, was the least of its problems, as it proved to be a very impractical and uncomfortable house to live

in. Four successive governors made do, but the arrival of Governor Arthur Kennedy in 1855 changed all that. Kennedy protested that the house was uninhabitable and approval was sought to build a replacement. The foundation stone for the new house was laid in 1859 and the building was completed in 1863 (at double the original budget), the old house being eventually demolished in the 1880s.

c. 1861

RIGHT: The new Government House under construction with the old house behind.

ABOVE: Sadly, Arthur Kennedy never got to live in his much wished for new residence and it was his successor, John Hampton, who became the first resident. Hampton arrived in 1862 and had a hand in many alterations to the original design. The result was a space fit for official and public entertainment – a major part of the governor's role – that included a small ballroom on the upper floor. This building served its purpose very well until the 1890s, when more space was needed for larger public gatherings. Drawings from 1897, signed by the Government Architect, John Grainger, show plans to add a new dining room and library, but these never came to fruition. However, a new ballroom and supper room were completed in 1899. Today Government House is the only one in Australia still to be on its original site, with those in other states having moved location at least once.

LANGLEY PARK
Perth's first commercial airstrip

BELOW: Langley Park was built on land reclaimed from the Swan River and was officially gazetted for the purpose of 'Parks, Gardens and Recreation' in December 1920. It is probably best known, however, as Perth's first commercial airstrip, pioneered by Major (later Sir) Norman Brearley, who used the park as his base when starting a civil aviation business in 1921. Brearley came to Perth in 1919 to give flying demonstrations to an adoring crowd. In 1920 he put a proposal to the Australian Commonwealth Government for a subsidised air mail service along the coast of Western Australia. As a result, West Australian Airways was Australia's first commercial air service, established 10 months before Qantas started operations in November 1922. This photo, taken shortly after air service commenced at Langley Park, shows Bristol Tourer biplanes belonging to West Australian Airways Ltd.

1922

BELOW: Because the park became boggy in winter, it was not an ideal location for a permanent airport and in November 1923 Brearley's operations moved to a site in Maylands. Close to the aircraft hangar was a pumping station built to improve the efficiency of the city's sewerage system. This facility, along with the rest of the system, was maintained by pump attendants, known as 'pumpies', who daily covered a circuit from Claisebrook to Subiaco on their bicycles to check operations. Named after Acting Lord Mayor, T.W. Langley, who opened the first section of Riverside Drive in 1937, the park is now a popular venue for both sporting and cultural events, particularly as a focal point for the city's Australia Day and Anzac Day commemorations. This photo is looking west towards Perth's central business district. The tallest building on the horizon is the 50-storey, 214-metre (702-foot), 108 St Georges Terrace (now South32 Tower). The small cottage-like building in the centre is one of the original pumping stations used to maintain Perth's sewerage system. The pumping stations were decommissioned in 1989 to make way for a central sewerage station.

1860

CAUSEWAY BRIDGE
Today's bridge is the third since 1843

ABOVE: In the early days of the Swan River Colony, the mud flats around Heirisson Island were a serious obstruction to road travel and discussion about bridging them commenced soon after settlement. Despite an urgent need, funds for a bridge were not available until 1839, when John Septimus Roe and Henry Trigg designed a bridge consisting of two timber spans and associated roadway, which was officially opened in May 1843. A toll was charged for almost everything crossing the causeway, including pedestrians, stock and vehicles. Exemptions were allowed only for officers and soldiers 'in proper uniform' and all mail carriers. By the 1860s the bridge was described as being in 'a moribund state', having been weakened by heavy use, frequent battering by vessels and being completely submerged during the floods of 1862.

1867

RIGHT: The second Causeway Bridge soon after opening.

ABOVE: A farmer was fined for causing an obstruction when the cattle he was driving took fright and wedged themselves between the bridge railings. Such incidents only added to the demands for a new and more substantial bridge. This was designed by Richard Roach Jewell and built using convict labour. The new bridge was similarly aligned to the previous one, but was 1 metre (3.3 feet) higher and divided into three, rather than two, spans. It opened for traffic in August 1865 and was officially opened by Governor Hampton in November 1867. Widened for a tramway in 1904 and again in 1932, by the late 1930s the bridge was only strong enough for a limited traffic-carrying capacity. War delayed the construction of a replacement bridge, but in 1949 a two-bridge, composite steel and concrete structure was built and opened for traffic in September 1952. The two-bridge structure, which continues to link the inner-city suburbs of East Perth and Victoria Park, is on the State Heritage Register and was awarded an Engineering Heritage Marker in 2012.

c. 1905

THE WACA

Western Australia's 'home of cricket'

ABOVE: The Western Australian Cricket Association (WACA) was established in November 1885. Soon after, it was granted a 999-year lease over 29 acres of swamp land to the east of the city on which to create a cricket ground. After the area had been drained and levelled, William Wise, gardener to the first Mayor of Perth, laid a turf wicket before the WACA Ground officially opened in 1893. The first match on the now hallowed turf wickets took place in February 1894. A year later, a grandstand seating 500 people was built, incorporating four dressing rooms and a dining room. Unfortunately, the beginning of the 20th century saw a period of financial instability for the Association and in 1907 the ground was under threat of being taken over by Perth City Council in settlement of debts.

ABOVE: Further financial difficulties led the Association to raise more funds by a charity cricket match with the Australian 1st XI in 1912 and in a further bid to stabilise finances, trotting races were introduced. Further excitement came in 1919, when Norman Brearley used the ground as a runway for the first flying demonstrations in Western Australia. These nearly ended in disaster when the plane almost got entangled in the electricity cables which encircled the ground. The ground's scoreboard was destroyed in a storm and replaced in 1954 with a mechanical one, which is still in use today, donated by the North West Murchison Cricket Association. With its modern concrete stands seating many thousands of people and high-intensity floodlighting, the ground appears a far cry from the halcyon days of club cricket, but Test matches at the WACA have helped to put Perth on the international map.

c. 1868

CLAISE BROOK

The quiet brook that flowed through bushland to the Swan River in East Perth is now part of a vibrant marina village

LEFT: The first mention of Claise Brook appears in an 1848 edition of the *Inquirer* newspaper, where it was announced that land at the mouth of the brook had been reserved for a water mill. In 1851 an abattoir was also established here, as it was an 'admirable distance out of town'. The name of the stream and cove was originally Clause's Brook, named after Frederick Clause, the surgeon who accompanied Captain James Stirling on his exploration of the Swan River in March 1827. Gradually, as Perth grew, the wetlands and surrounding bush to the north and east of the city were systematically drained, with much of the water being diverted into Claise Brook.

RIGHT: In the latter part of the 19th century much of the area of East Perth surrounding Claise Brook was industrialised, with East Perth Gas Works, the railway yards and a sewage works being built there. As a result, the brook was used as an open sewer to carry effluent to the river and became heavily polluted. With a decline in the industrial use of the area from the late 1960s onwards, and with a marked reduction in its population, Claisebrook Cove became a deserted and desolate part of East Perth. In the early 1990s an urban regeneration program was undertaken to transform the place into a vibrant city village of residential and retail properties, surrounding an enlarged Claisebrook Cove marina. As for the brook itself, it still runs, but for much of its length in an underground culvert. Trafalgar Bridge, the large footbridge crossing the cove, is at the heart of what is now known as Claisebrook Village. Beyond Trafalgar Bridge, on the other side of the river, is Perth's new 6,000-seat stadium, currently under construction and due to open in 2018.

1894

ST MARY'S CATHEDRAL

The cathedral grew and changed with each stage of its construction

ABOVE: The construction of the first Roman Catholic church in Perth, St John's, started in January 1844. A year later the Catholic Diocese of Perth was formed and St John's Church was elevated to the status of cathedral. By the early 1860s the number of Roman Catholics in Perth had grown to the extent that a new and larger cathedral became necessary. This was built on a site that had originally been intended for the principal Anglican church in Perth, but was considered too far from the centre of St Georges Terrace to be practical. The foundation stone for the new cathedral, which was designed by Benedictine Oblate Brother Joseph Ascione, was laid by Bishop Rosendo Salvado in February 1863. Alas, a lack of funds retarded progress and it was not completed until 1865.

ABOVE: Between 1897 and 1905 various alterations were made to the building, including the addition of a steeple, pinnacles and gargoyles to the bell tower, a porch and electricity. In the 1920s, under the dynamic Archbishop Clune, various schemes were considered to complete the cathedral, including one by the priest-architect John Hawes for a huge Romanesque building. However, financial constraints dictated that just a new sanctuary and east end could be built and the extension was blessed by Bishop Clune in May 1930. This created a very imposing Norman Gothic building that served its community well. By the beginning of the 21st century the cathedral was again creaking at the seams and so work began in August 2006 to create a new, larger nave area in the middle of the cathedral. The newly enlarged cathedral was re-consecrated by the Archbishop of Perth in December 2009.

ST GEORGE'S HALL

Only the classical facade of this former theatre remains

c. 1890

LEFT: Today it seems strange that a firm of solicitors should decide Perth needed a theatre, but it was the long-established legal firm of Stone and Burt who were the prime movers in the construction of a multi-purpose hall that could be used for theatrical productions. As a result, St George's Hall was built in 1879 with a portico said to be a copy of the Lyceum Theatre in London. The unfinished hall was first used as a public auction room in August 1879, with the official opening occurring just over a month later. The new hall clearly gave great satisfaction, as the *West Australian Times* was able to report: 'Messrs Stone and Burt are the proprietors of St George's Hall, and these gentlemen have spared no expense to adapt the building to the purposes for which it was designed.'

BELOW: Until the opening of the Theatre Royal in 1897, St George's Hall was a popular venue for much music and drama performances and an important part of Perth's cultural life. For a short while in 1907 it was renamed the Sixpenny Picture Palace and used as a cinema. After this the name changed and the hall was used mainly for dances. In March 1913, however, a very significant occasion in the history of education in Western Australia took place in the hall when the first meeting of the University of Western Australia's Convocation was held there. Soon after this, the building was taken over by the government and used for administrative purposes. Apart from the facade, the hall was demolished in 1986 to make way for a new Lands Administration office, which in turn was removed in 2004 to be replaced by a new District Court building.

c. 1932

TRANBY HOUSE / PENINSULA FARM

One of the first farms and earliest homes of the Swan River Colony

ABOVE: When Joseph Hardey and his family settled on what is now known as the Maylands Peninsula in 1830, he named their wattle-and-daub, thatch-roofed farmhouse Tranby, after the ship that brought them to Western Australia. Despite being some 30 metres (98 feet) from the river bank, the house got washed away by a flood just months after being completed. Undaunted, Hardey built another one, which was washed away six years later. For a few years the family gave up and lived on another property they owned in York, but clearly the close proximity of his Swan River site to Perth drew Hardey back, for in 1838 he recorded in his diary that he had purchased bricks and wood for a new house and by June 1839 it was complete.

ABOVE: The Hardey family continued to farm at Tranby until the beginning of the 20th century, after which the property was sold on twice and became known as Peninsula Farm. During the 1960s the land was purchased by the Bond Corporation with a view to creating a large housing development. One of the planning conditions for the development was that Tranby House should be restored in consultation with the

National Trust and the property was vested with them in 1977. Since that date, Tranby House has been subject to many phases of conservation and is open to the public from Friday to Sunday each week. Now the oldest residence in the metropolitan area, the house tells the story of those hard early days when settlers were trying to survive in a fledgling colony, situated in a strange and distant land.

1926

ASCOT RACECOURSE
The 'grand old lady' of Australian racecourses

122

LEFT: Given that many who settled in the Swan River Colony were from the higher ranks of British society, it is not surprising that the 'sport of kings', horse racing, featured in the sporting calendar from an early date. In addition to draught horses, early settlers brought with them thoroughbreds and the first recorded race meeting took place in Fremantle in October 1833. In 1848 a race was held on land owned by John Hardey near the Swan River, but Hardey's brother believed horse racing to be the 'gun shot of the devil', so permission for further races was withdrawn. T.R.C. Walters donated land from his adjoining property which became Ascot Racecourse, where the erection of a grandstand in 1903 brought to an end the holiday custom of picnicking on the 'flat' in the centre of the track.

ABOVE: Ascot became the headquarters for horse racing in Western Australia in 1917, at which time the course was given a number of additional facilities, including a ledger stand, steward's stand and dining rooms. During World War II the racecourse was used as an army camp, which gave temporary accommodation to American soldiers, and racing was confined to the second Saturday of the month. Parts of the original grandstand, including the cast-iron roof support columns, were incorporated into a major refurbishment and upgrading of the building, which took place in 1969. Ascot Racecourse is probably best known for the Perth Cup, which now takes place on New Year's Day and is a popular event in Perth's social calendar. The race was first held in 1887 and ran over a 3.2-kilometre (2-mile) course, the first winner being the appropriately named First Prince.

c. 1905

OLD MILL, SOUTH PERTH

Its surroundings have changed beyond recognition

LEFT: William Shenton built a windmill on Point Belches, South Perth, because of its close proximity to central Perth and ease of access to Fremantle and Guildford via the Swan River. The foundation stone for the building was laid by Governor Stirling in 1835 and two years later the mill was ready for use. At the time, the Colonial Civil Engineer, Henry Reveley, whose own water mill in Perth had failed dismally, peevishly remarked that it was 'a miserable toy, which will never do much'. Sadly, Reveley was right. A new owner converted it to steam power in the 1850s, but this was not viable either, so in 1879 a colourful South Perth resident, Thomas (Satan) Brown leased the buildings and converted them into a hotel and picnic ground called the Alta Gardens.

LEFT AND ABOVE: Thomas Brown's scheme was also a financial failure and the site was successively used as a residence, wine saloon and poultry farm until acquired by the government in 1929. In the late 1950s the Old Mill was in danger of being demolished to make way for the Kwinana Freeway, but was saved thanks to the intervention of the local community. The Old Mill and its cottage were granted to the City of South Perth to commemorate the centenary of the founding of South Perth. Fully restored, the mill became a folk museum, until passing into the care of the National Trust in 1992. In more recent times an extensive restoration has taken place, returning the Old Mill and cottage to a close approximation to their original appearance. In the view above the mill is partially obscured by the busy Kwinana Freeway taking traffic between central Perth and South Perth.

1870

NARROWS BRIDGE

On completion it was the largest precast, pre-stressed concrete bridge in the world

ABOVE: While an important thoroughfare for the early settlers, the Swan River was also a great inconvenience when it came to getting from one bank to the other. As early as 1849 there was the suggestion that a bridge be built across the entrance to Perth Water, known as the Narrows. This suggestion induced the leader writer for the *Perth Gazette* to proclaim the idea to be, 'A scheme so ridiculous and extravagant that it could never be entertained for one moment, save by the most inveterate theorist.' Nothing further was done about a bridge until the population of South Perth rapidly increased during the first gold rush of the 1890s. At this time, attempts were made to establish a pontoon ferry service for vehicles across the Narrows, but these were unsuccessful. The photo on right shows the newly constructed Narrows Bridge, with Matilda Bay and Nedlands in the distance.

1960

ABOVE: Eventually, work on a new bridge spanning the Narrows and connecting the northern and southern suburbs began in 1954. There was much public consternation over the choice of site as it was felt the bridge would ruin picturesque views. Veteran campaigner Bessie Rischbieth protested by wading ankle-deep into the river and standing defiantly in front of the bulldozers. Despite protests, the Narrows Bridge went ahead and was opened in November 1959. The six-lane bridge, which was said to be the largest precast, pre-stressed concrete bridge in the world, formed part of the new 4-kilometre (2.5-mile) long Kwinana Freeway. During the construction it was announced that the bridge would be known as Golden West Bridge. This caused much amusement as this was also the name of a popular soft drink and so the name was quietly jettisoned. A second road bridge was added in 2001 and a railway bridge, carrying the Perth to Mandurah line, was built in between them in 2007.

c. 1910

OLD SWAN BREWERY

Described by the Heritage Council as 'the finest connected group of late-Victorian and early 20th-century brewery buildings in Australia'

LEFT: Frank Sherwood established the famous Swan Brewery in 1857 and built his brew house in Bazaar Terrace (the riverside road between Mill and William Streets), where a very pure water source was to be found. He then placed an advertisement in the *Perth Gazette*: 'The Public are respectfully informed that after the first day of November next, they may be supplied with superior Pale Ale.' After Sherwood's death, the brewery was leased to Ferguson & Mumme, who moved it in 1879 to the site shown here at the foot of Mount Eliza where a flour mill had been. The business took off and by the beginning of World War I it was producing nearly 40 per cent of the beer brewed in Western Australia. This view of the brewery, taken from Mount Eliza, shows Mill Point in South Perth behind.

ABOVE: In the period between the two wars, the Swan Brewery continued to flourish, introducing its famous Swan Lager in the 1940s. During the 1960s a very popular annual feature was the external lighting display. Each year a different ship was depicted in coloured lights on the river side of the brewery site. The brewery was relocated to modern premises in Canning Vale in 1978, which was followed by a great deal of controversy and protest over the use of the old site. Eventually, most of the outbuildings were removed, with the main building being completely restored and adapted for reuse as a restaurant, micro-brewery, function centre, offices and apartments. This historic building continues to be a popular spot due to its magnificent views of the city and the Swan River. The Narrows Bridge on the left, which connects South Perth with central Perth, was opened in 1959.

1940

CRAWLEY BATHS

A modern swimming complex replaced the baths when Perth hosted the 1962 British Empire and Commonwealth Games

LEFT: Crawley Baths were built to replace the very muddy-bottomed City Baths on the Esplanade. A site on Mounts Bay Road with a sandy river bed was chosen, but being at the foot of Mount Eliza, the choice provoked much opposition. Opponents felt people on the hill's slopes would be able to look down on swimmers dressing and undressing. Ignoring this opposition, a lido was built at a cost of £5,000. The baths were opened in February 1914 by the Premier, John Scaddan, followed by a swimming carnival and life-saving display. This new facility provoked the comment, 'At last Perth has the chance to achieve greatness' from the *West Australian* newspaper. Said to have been the largest enclosed body of water in the Southern Hemisphere, the pool was upgraded to Olympic dimensions in 1933. This view is looking west towards houses on the lower slopes of Mount Eliza.

ABOVE AND RIGHT: Countless thousands of children learnt to swim at Crawley Baths, with many having the unpleasant experience of ploughing through the large shoals of brown jellyfish which frequented the pool in warmer weather. When it was announced that the British Empire and Commonwealth Games were coming to Perth in 1962, a modern swimming complex was built at Beatty Park and Crawley Baths were demolished in 1964. To commemorate the site of the old pool (of which nothing now remains) the City of Perth commissioned Perth sculptor Tony Jones to create the figure of a woman (shown right) about to dive into the water some 15 metres (49 feet) off-shore. The sculpture was unveiled in 2007, since when it has frequently been dressed in a variety of costumes to suit all occasions. (The cormorant is not part of the sculpture!)

1949

MATILDA BAY

Still a perfect spot to relax and enjoy the view

ABOVE: Before European colonisation, the area that became Matilda Bay was an important estuarine food source for the Noongar people. In March 1827 Captain James Stirling explored the Swan River and described the area as 'amongst the most beautiful of its kind I have ever seen'. It was named Matilda Bay after the wife of John Septimus Roe, Surveyor General of the Swan River Colony, but has also been known as Eliza, Currie's, Sutherland's and Crawley Bay. Considered very remote from Perth in the early days, the area was initially owned by Captain Mark Currie, the first Harbour Master of Fremantle, who sold it on to Henry Sutherland. Sutherland built a house on the estate and changed the name to Crawley Park. His house still exists on the campus of the University of Western Australia. This view of Matilda Bay is looking south towards Pelican Point.

ABOVE: The construction of the tram line to Nedlands made Matilda Bay more accessible to the masses, and in the 20th century it became a favourite Sunday picnicking spot for residents of both Perth and Subiaco. Occasional informal sailing regattas in the bay led to the formation of the Royal Perth Yacht Club in 1865. For its first 90 years the club was based in Perth, but in 1953 it moved to its present site on Matilda Bay. During World War II the bay became an important location in the defence of Australia, with 60 to 70 US Navy Catalinas being stationed here. Today Matilda Bay is still as popular as ever for water-based leisure activities and has accessible paths for pedestrians and cyclists. Overlooking the river and the city, with Kings Park as a backdrop, Matilda Bay is still a perfect spot to just sit, relax and enjoy the view.

1932

WINTHROP HALL, UNIVERSITY OF WESTERN AUSTRALIA

The first non-fee-paying university in the British Empire

ABOVE: Thanks to the efforts of Sir John Winthrop Hackett, proprietor and editor of the *West Australian* newspaper, the University of Western Australia was established in 1911 as the first non-fee-paying university in the British Empire. The university opened in 1913 with 184 students who were taught in a collection of wooden and corrugated iron buildings on Irwin Street in the city centre – a group which became known as 'Tin-Pan Alley'. As the university grew, it became necessary to create a proper, custom-built campus with all necessary facilities. In 1929, thanks to an enormous bequest from Sir Winthrop Hackett's estate, a 51-hectare site in Crawley was acquired and building work commenced. One of the new buildings was the magnificent, Mediterranean-style Winthrop Hall, completed in 1932.

1920

RIGHT: The original university buildings, known as 'Tin-Pan Alley', on the corner of Irwin Street and St Georges Terrace.

ABOVE: Known as the jewel in the crown of the University of Western Australia, Winthrop Hall is permanently entered into the Register of Heritage Places. One of the Irwin Street buildings was moved to the Crawley campus and is still in use today as the Convocation Council Room, university archives and cricket club pavilion. After World War II, with government encouragement, the number of enrolments to the university increased dramatically and precipitated several flurries of building work around the campus to accommodate the additional students. As well as the old Irwin Street building, the university also occupies the two-storey Crawley Park Homestead, built in 1846 for Henry Sutherland, the Colonial Treasurer. Adapted for teaching use, this building now houses the university's School of Indigenous Studies. With an international reputation for its teaching and research, the university currently has around 40,000 students.

COTTESLOE BEACH
'The Brighton of the West'

1920

LEFT: The district of Cottesloe was given its name in September 1886, in honour of Baron Cottesloe, brother of Captain C.H. Fremantle. Prior to this, the first British settler in the area was John Butler who had a 250-acre agricultural holding. His first crop was barley, which he used to brew beer to sell from his home (known as the 'Half-Way House'). With the opening of the Perth to Fremantle railway in 1881, the area became more accessible and resulted in a rush to take up land in this pleasant seaside suburb. With the rise in popularity of going to the seaside as a form of recreation, Cottesloe became Perth's favourite beach and was further developed as ever-increasing crowds visited at weekends. This view is looking north over Cottesloe beach and includes the old Cottesloe jetty and the Indiana Tea House, which started life in 1910 as an ice-cream parlour.

BELOW: Cottesloe became known as 'the Brighton of the West', probably because of the construction of a jetty in 1906. News of the jetty spread and the beach became even more popular for sea bathing. The growing trend of mixed bathing met with grave disapproval in some quarters and so the council put up a notice prescribing the type of costumes to be worn by bathers. Three concrete pylons were built to anchor a shark net following a fatal attack in 1925. Two of these were destroyed by storms and the other remains to this day as a popular marker for swimmers. Increasing maintenance problems with the jetty led to its demolition in 1952 in a spectacular gelignite explosion. The original Indiana Tea House has altered over the years and was redeveloped into its present form in 1996. Today it is a restaurant known as Indiana Cottesloe Beach.

1940

CITY BEACH

Named after the ocean suburb nearest to the city centre

ABOVE: In 1834 Henry Trigg was granted 500 acres of land that had an easily quarried Tamala Limestone formation. Having developed a very successful quarrying and lime-burning business on the property, Trigg consolidated his holding to form a 1,235-acre estate which became known as the Limekilns Estate. In 1917 Perth City Council purchased the estate with a view to creating an up-to-date seaside town, modelled on the British 'garden city' principle of urban planning developed in the late 19th century by Sir Ebenezer Howard. The town, situated close to the ocean, was to embody all the latest planning principles, with ample leisure facilities included. The council allocated finance to commence work in 1928 and named the beachside suburb City Beach.

ABOVE: Perth City Council extended Cambridge Street through the newly acquired Limekilns Estate to the ocean. The single track road was built of jarrah planks laid lengthwise on railway sleepers, infilled with limestone aggregate. This road was upgraded and metalled in 1951 and renamed Oceanic Drive. In 1939, to make access to the area even easier, work commenced on the construction of the West Coast Highway, which connects Cottesloe to Scarborough via City Beach. With its uninterrupted view over the Indian Ocean, City Beach remains a very popular destination for locals and tourists. The City to Surf marathon, which has taken place every August since 1975, is now the second largest officially timed race in the Southern Hemisphere, with over 50,000 participants. After winding its way out of the city, the run finishes at City Beach.

c. 1945

SUBIACO OVAL

A Western Australian sporting institution

LEFT: The first game of Australian Rules Football in WA was played between Subiaco and Fremantle on the ground which later became Subiaco Oval. It took place on the 'Sand Patch' on Mueller Road (now Roberts Road) in July 1896. The ground proved less than suitable for the game and after about a year the team moved to a ground in West Subiaco (now Shenton Park), which was also found to be impractical, as it was frequently submerged by the adjoining swamp in winter. In 1906 Subiaco Council announced plans to improve Mueller Road Reserve in order to create a ground suitable for football and cricket. On Saturday 18 April 1908 Subiaco hosted a practice game with Cottesloe Football Club, which was the first recorded game on what was to become one of Australia's most famous sporting arenas.

ABOVE: The ground became the headquarters of the West Australian Football League in 1936, since when all finals and state games have been played at Subiaco Oval. Over the years, the ground has changed out of all recognition. Various stands have come and gone and player facilities have been improved numerous times. Today the crowds average around 40,000; a far cry from the 6,000 who packed the Oval at its opening in 1908. Only the entrance and turnstiles, built in 1935 to commemorate the Jubilee of King George V, remain as a reminder of past footballing eras. A new and larger stadium in Burswood opened in 2018 and the terraces of the Subiaco Oval no longer resound to the chanting of Eagles and Dockers supporters. The area around the ground is to be redeveloped, with the pitch reopened for use by local sport and community groups.

c. 1914

HYDE PARK

Named after London's famous park

ABOVE: Hyde Park was once part of a natural wetland system covering an extensive area north of Perth. Prior to European settlement, the swamp's lush vegetation and wildlife provided water, shelter and food for the Aboriginal people. To European settlers it was known as Third Swamp, which used to flood and cause serious problems. Draining the swamp commenced in 1873, but had to be stopped because

nearby wells began to dry up. In 1896, largely through the efforts of Lyall Hall, a local auctioneer and land agent, the Executive Council recommended that Third Swamp Reserve should be turned into public gardens. The area was gazetted for that use in September 1897 and creation of the gardens began the following year with the construction of roads to define the southern and western boundaries.

ABOVE: Soon after opening, a picket fence was erected to stop cattle and horses roaming into the park. A grant of £1,000 was made in 1899 for improvements, including planting 600 trees, and in the same year the park was named Hyde Park, after the famous park in London. A practice cricket pitch was constructed in 1906 and the perimeter planted with pine trees in 1912. A roadway through the centre of the park was built in 1913, but public opposition caused it to be turned into a walkway dividing the lake in two. A bandstand was built during World War I and Jacaranda trees were planted in the early 1920s. The park became somewhat neglected in the 1960s, but was given a much-need facelift and is once again one of Perth's most popular parks.

INDEX

Albert Facey House 75
Allendale Square 31
Alta Gardens 124
Ambassadors Theatre 94–95
AMP Chambers 30–31
Annabella's Nightclub 21
Art Gallery of Western Australia 79
Arthur Head 41
Ascalon 105
Ascot Racecourse 122–123
Ascione, Joseph 116
Avenue of Honour 44
Barrack Square 88, 99
Barrack Street 10, 11, 14, 75, 87, 88–89, 98–99, 100, 101
Barrack Street Bridge 86–87
Barrack Street Jetty 22, 24
Barracks Arch 49
Barracks Guard House 100
Basil Kirke Studios 27
Bazaar Terrace 129
Beatty Park 131
Beaufort Street 81, 85, 87
Bell Tower 13, 25, 99
Bernales, Claude de 68, 70
Bishop Hale's School 36–37
Blackett, Edmund 104
Boan, Benjamin 57
Boan, Harry 57
Boans' Department Store 57, 73
Bon Marche Arcade 88, 89
Bon Marche drapery store 103
Brass Monkey Hotel 57
Brearley, Sir Norman 108, 113
Brewer Street 85
Broken Hill 51
Brookfield Place 33, 35
Brown, Thomas (Satan) 124, 125
Busy Bee Arcade 72
Butler, John 137
Cambridge Street 139
Canning Vale 129
Capitol Theatre 26–27
Cathedral Avenue 101
Cathedral Square 103
Causeway Bridge 110–111
Cavanagh, Michael 57
Cenotaph, The 44, 45
Central Arcade 72–73, 75
Central Government Offices 12, 13, 99, 100–101, 103
Central Hotel 75
Central Park 91
Citibank House 10–11, 99
City Beach 138–139
City Markets 60–61
Claise Brook 114–115
Claisebrook Cove 115
Claisebrook Cove Marina 115
Claisebrook Village 115
Clause, Frederick 114
Cleland, John 34
Cloisters, The 36–37
Clune, Archbishop 117
CMLA Building 7
Cockburn Sound 6
Cole, Henry 12, 99
Cole's Jetty 99
Colonial School 7
Commissariat Stores 12, 17, 18–19
Commonwealth Bank Building 7, 75
Convocation Council Room 135
Cooke, William 40
Coolgardie 57
Cottesloe, Baron 137

Cottesloe Beach 136–137
Court of Contemplation 45
Crawley 134, 135
Crawley Baths 23, 130–131
Crawley Park Homestead 135
Currie, Mark 132
Curtin House 85
Curtin University 35
Dadich, Drago 55
Darling, Eliza 43
Darling Ranges 41
De Baun, John 29, 51
District Court Building 119
Dixon, William 28
Doyle, Stuart 94
Drummond, James 12
Eagle Tavern 51
East Perth Gas Works 115
Eastern Goldfield 7
Edgley, Michael 52
Edward VII, King 43
Elizabeth II, Queen 73
Elizabeth Quay 21, 23, 24–25
Enrolled Pensioner Force 38, 39
Esplanade, The 14, 21, 26, 70, 131
Esplanade Kiosk 20–21, 23
Esplanade Recreation Ground 20, 25
Esplanade Reserve 23, 24–25
Exchange Plaza 15
Fallen Soldiers' Memorial 44
Fisher, Andrew 85
Flame of Remembrance 45
Florence Hummerston Day Care Centre 21
Forrest, Alexander 13
Forrest, John 40, 43
Forrest Chase Shopping Centre 73
Forrest Place 72–73, 75
Fraser, Malcolm 43
Freemason's Hotel 28–29
Fremantle, C.H. 137
Fremantle to Guildford railway line 57, 58, 76, 77, 87, 137
Fremantle Harbour 41
General Post Office building 73, 74–75
George IV, King 8
Giles, Ernest 97
Gledden Building 7, 67
Government Astronomer's House 40, 41, 43
Government Gardens 12–13
Government Geology Building 81
Government House 7, 18, 106–107
Governor's Jetty 12
Grainger, John 19, 107
Grainger, Percy 19
Great Western Hotel 56–57
Gun Alley 70
Hackett Hall 81
Hale, Matthew Blagden 36, 104
Half-Way House 137
Hall, Lyall 142
Hampton, John 96, 107, 111
Hardey, John 123
Hardey, Joseph 63, 120
Harmony of Minerals 13
Hawes, John 117
Hay, Robert William 91
Hay Street 17, 51, 63, 66–67, 68, 89, 90–91, 92, 93, 103
Heardsman's Lake 31
Heirisson Island 110
Hill, Kerry 103
His Majesty's Theatre 7, 64–65, 93
Hobbs, Smith & Forbes 32

Holocaust Memorial 13
Horseshoe Bridge 58–59, 61
Hotel Metropole 92–93
Howard, Robert 58
Howick, Viscount 91
Howick Street 91
Hummerston, Florence 21
Hyde Park 142–143
Indiana Cottesloe Beach 137
Indiana Tea House 137
Irwin Street 17, 134
James, Greg 55
James Street 35, 78
Jewell, Richard Roach 7, 36, 38, 63, 96, 100, 111
Johnson, G.R. 22
Jones, Tony 131
Kalgoorlie Miner 66
Kennedy, Arthur 106, 107
King George's Terrace 8
King's Head Hotel 28
Kings Park 42–43, 44, 45, 46–47
Kings Park Botanic Gardens 13, 45
Kohler, Edward 69
Kwinana Freeway 39, 49, 125, 127
Land Titles Building 7, 101
Langley, T.W. 109
Langley Park 108–109
Law Chambers building 103
Leake, George 46
Leake Memorial 46–47
Leeder, William 28
Leeders Hotel 28
Liberty Theatre 89
Liebe, Gustav 65
Limekilns Estate 138, 139
Linton, James 46
London Court 70–71
Malloy, Thomas 65, 92, 93
market gardens 48–49
Marylands Peninsula 120
Matilda Bay 126, 132–133
May Drive 44
Maylands 109
McNess Royal Arcade 7
McNess's ironmongers shop 96
Melbourne Hotel 50–51, 65
Melbourne Road 51
Midland Junction 76
Mill Point 129
Mill Street 36, 37, 129
Milligan Street 51
Mount Eliza 40, 43, 48, 129, 131
Mount Hospital 49
Mount Lawley 88
Mounts Bay Road 48–49, 131
Mouritzen, Christian 26
Mueller Road 141
Murchison Goldfield 7
Murray, Lord 7
Murray Street 68, 69, 72
Narrows Bridge 49, 126–127
National Bank of Australasia Building 10
Nedlands 126, 133
Newspaper House 32–33
Nicholson's Music Centre 89
Northam 76
Northbridge 54, 59, 61
Oceanic Drive 139
Old Court House 12, 16–17, 18
Old Court House Law Museum 17
Old Mill 124–125
Old Perth Gaol 76, 81, 87
Old Swan Brewery 128–129
Oldham, John 47

Oldham and Cox 30
Osborne Park 33
Padbury Buildings 73
Palace Hotel 28–29
Parliament House 39
Pelican Point 132
Peninsula Farm 120–121
Pensioner Barracks 38–39
Perth Arena 52–53
Perth Boys' School 34–35, 58
Perth Boys' and Girls' School 78–79
Perth Central Bus Station 61
Perth Church of England Collegiate School 36
Perth City Baths 22–23, 24, 99, 131
Perth City Library 103, 105
Perth City Link 53, 59, 61
Perth Cultural Centre 79
Perth Drill Hall 17
Perth Entertainment Centre 52–53
Perth Gazette 17, 126, 129
Perth Gazette and Western Australian Journal 32
Perth Hospital 70
Perth Institute of Contemporary Arts 78–79
Perth Observatory 40–41, 46
Perth Park 42–43
Perth Railway Station 57, 60, 70, 72, 76–77
Perth Technical College 79
Perth Technical School 35, 46
Perth Water 44, 126
Perth Yacht Club 24, 25
Perth Zoo 23
Piccadilly Arcade 68–69
Pioneer Women's Memorial Fountain 45
Point Belches 124
Pool of Reflection 45
Queen's Gardens 104
Railway Hotel 88
Reveley, Henry 17, 18, 106, 124
Rischbieth, Bessie 127
Riverside Drive 23, 109
Roberts Road 141
Robinson, Sir William 104
Roe, John Septimus 43, 110, 132
Roe, Matilda 132
Royal Hotel 61
Royal Perth Golf Club 23
Rush Church 17
Russell, John 54
Russell Square 54–55
St Brigid's Catholic Church 54
St George's Cathedral 14, 103, 104–105
St George's Chambers 102–103, 104, 105
St George's Hall 118–119
St Georges Terrace 8–9, 10, 11, 14, 24, 28, 30, 32, 33, 34, 36, 49, 75, 78, 81, 91, 100, 116, 134
St John's Church 116
St John's University Hostel 37
St Mary's Cathedral 116–117
Salvado, Rosendo 116
Sandford, William 34
Scaddan, John 131
Shearer Memorial Hall 85
Shenton, George 63
Shenton, William 124
Shenton Park 141
Sherwood, Frank 129
Sherwood Court 24
South Perth 22, 23, 24, 99, 124, 125, 126, 129
Spanda 25
State Buildings 11

State Library of Western Australia 79
State Theatre Centre 79
State War Memorial 44–45
Stiles, James 93
Stirling, James 7, 17, 106, 114, 124, 132
Stirling Gardens 12–13, 47
Subiaco Oval 140–141
Supreme Court 18–19
Sutherland, Henry 132, 135
Swan Barracks 82–83
Swan Bells 13, 25, 99
Swan River 6, 7, 12, 48, 99, 108, 114, 120, 123, 124, 126, 129, 132
Swan River Colony 6, 10, 17, 18, 34, 43, 110, 123
T&G Chambers 10–11, 99
Talbot Hobbs, Sir John 10, 14, 44
Temple Court Cabaret 26–27
Temple-Poole, George 26, 40, 76, 82, 83, 101
Theatre Royal 65, 92–93, 119
Third Swamp Reserve 142
Town Hall 7, 12, 66, 67, 88, 89, 91, 96–97
Trades Hall 84–85
Trafalgar Bridge 115
Tranby House 120–121
Transit Circle Building 40
Treasure, Brian 52
Treasury Building 75
Trigg, Henry 110, 138
Trollope, Anthony 48
Twiss, Horace 91
Twiss Street 90–91
United Services Hotel 8, 9
United Service Tavern Hotel 10
Unity Theatre 85
University of Western Australia 37, 119, 132, 134–135
Victoria, Queen 7, 81, 105
Victoria Hotel 54
Victoria Library 81
WACA, The 112–113
Walters, T.R.C. 123
Wardle, Thomas 27
Weld, Frederick 14, 43
Weld Chambers 8, 9
Weld Club 14–15, 99
Wellington Street 60, 61, 72, 75, 88
Wembley Downs 37
Wesfarmers House 27
Wesley Arcade and Tower 63
Wesley Church 62–63, 66, 67, 91
Western Australia Women's Suffrage Memorial 45
West Australian 32, 33, 37, 57, 67, 131, 134
West Australian Times 119
West Australian Botanic Gardens 47
West Australian Chambers 32
West Coast Highway 139
Western Australian Museum 58, 79, 80–81, 87
White, Henry 94
Whiteman, Lew 31
William Street 26, 28, 30, 32, 60, 63, 72, 87, 91, 129
William Street Jetty 22, 24, 99
Winthrop Hackett, Sir John 134
Winthrop Hall 134–135
Wise, William 112
Wittenoom, Edward 78
Wolf, William 65
Working Men's Institute 87
Yagan Square 59, 61

OTHER AVAILABLE TITLES

ISBN 9781911595601

ISBN 9781909815322

ISBN 9781909815315

ISBN 9781910496732

ISBN 9781910496749

ISBN 9781910904794

ISBN 9781911216827

ISBN 9781910904091

ISBN 9781911216926